# The Red-Eye Fever

# Also By

# Elise Dallemagne-Cookson

THE FILMMAKER
**a novel**
THE OMBÚ TREE
**a novel**
THE BEARDED LION WHO ROARS
**"Simba Mandefu Mabe"**
**a memoir**

# The Red-Eye Fever

## Adventures in the Belgian Congo

Elise Dallemagne-Cookson

**To order additional copies of this book, contact:**
Xlibris Corporation
1-888-795-4274
www.Xlibris.com
Orders@Xlibris.com
16256

# Contents

For

MAGDELEINE DALLEMAGNE

My Granddaughter

# AUTHOR'S NOTE

THIS IS A true story, transcribed from notes I made at the time the events described occurred. It is about crocodile hunting in the former Belgian Congo—my first African adventure. Fresh from New York, I began my Congo career by participating in the slaying of the monster crocodile of the Kwango River, known as El Diablo. This infamous 175-year-old crocodile had been preying on the people for many years and was known to have consumed at least fifty inhabitants during its lifetime.

This adventure was to be followed by many others in that country, now called the Democratic Republic of the Congo. It tells of the extraordinary people I met and the expeditions into the interior that I participated in when the Congo was preparing to take its place in African history as the first colony south of the Sahara to win its independence.

Elise Dallemagne-Cookson
Cherry Valley, New York
2002

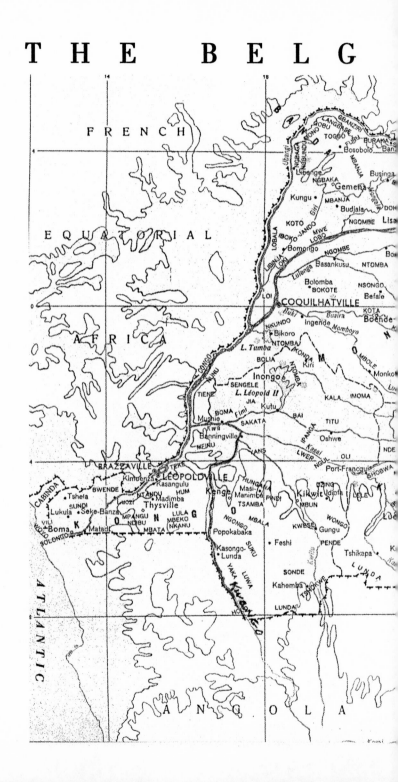

# 1.

## LEOPOLDVILLE
## BELGIAN CONGO
## 1959

"I WANT TO show you Leopoldville," Claude Stylo said. "Would you like to see the zoo tomorrow?"

"A zoo? *Here?*" I was incredulous. "The whole place is a zoo. The entire country."

There was a glint of pleasure in his eyes. "You're right. But, you see, most of the Belgians living in Leopoldville never get out into the countryside. They're too scared. And certainly their children never do. So the government has to show them at least one gorilla, lion, baboon, a few chimps, some monkeys or a crocodile before they head back home."

He laughed for the first time since we had met the week before, which had been at the welcoming dinner the U.S. Consul General had given me as his newly-arrived public affairs assistant. Claude had been introduced as the manager of the Banque du Congo Belge, and in a whispered aside by the wife of the director of Unilever, Mrs. de Coster, I was also informed that he was the most eligible bachelor in Leopoldville. This did not impress me. I had not left Hollywood, New York and Washington for the Belgian Congo in search of romance. In fact, the Belgian Congo was the last place in the world I expected, or wanted, to find it.

"Okay," I agreed. "Why not? There's not much else to do around here on a Saturday afternoon, is there?"

He picked me up the following day at my hotel, the Regina, where I was staying until I could find an apartment. He had a white MG, which he drove, I thought, altogether too fast for a sports car. I remembered Mrs. de Coster also telling me that his wife had been killed in a car accident the year before. "Please be good to him," she had whispered in my ear. "He's still mourning her loss."

The zoo was located not far from the center of Leopoldville and occupied several acres carved out of the jungle. It was deserted except for a few captive specimens of jungle life. Several healthy-looking lions prowled angrily about in a cage, while monkeys chattered mockingly in the trees above them, taunting, swinging in freedom from limb to limb, defying gravity. Farther on an adult chimpanzee was attached by a chain around its neck to an overhead rope strung between two trees and was pacing, pacing, up and down like a madman in an insane asylum. He held out his arms to me, his eyes pleading for release. "Don't go near him," Claude warned. "He might look harmless, but he's capable of crushing your bones in his embrace. Come, let's see the gorilla," he urged. "You'll like him."

He was a colossal coal-black male mountain gorilla, who hurried over to the bars of his cage as we approached. He looked at me with infinitely sad, almost human eyes, as though to say, "I know you. What are you doing here? Look at me. Have pity on me."

"Watch this," Claude said, taking a cigarette out of his pack. He held it out to the gorilla, which reached through his bars with one thick padded paw and delicately took it from Claude. He then carefully put it between his lips and pressed his gigantic face close enough to the bars for Claude to light it for him. The gorilla inhaled with great satisfaction, then turned his back on us and ambled over to a corner of his enclosure, where he settled himself down to enjoy his cigarette in private and smoked with all the languid gestures of an opium pipe addict.

"*Amazing.*"

Claude shook his head and looking rather sad murmured, "Reminds me of some people I know."

In his early thirties, Claude had the delicate features of a young boy whose development had been arrested around the age of twelve. He was also exceedingly tall and thin and walked as though he had a steel rod in his back holding him up—as rigid as a tree in a crowded forest, undernourished and deprived of sunlight. Indeed, for one who had spent years in the tropics, his skin was unusually pale. He gestured a great deal with nervous hands, and I couldn't decide if he was shy or just plain high-strung.

We sat down on a nearby stone bench. Fascinated, I continued to watch the gorilla, while Claude kept his eyes on me. "Your face appears to be clearing up. The black and blue fading. Somewhat," he said.

My hand flew instantly to my left cheek, and I began to massage the blood clot, as large as a pigeon's egg, that had now lodged there under the skin between my lips and the lobe of my ear. "You think so?"

"It must have been terrible."

"It was."

"When I saw you arrive at the Consul General's residence, I was astounded. Everyone was. It was not what we expected."

I smiled. "Oh, no? And what did you expect?"

"The usual mousy type sent out by Washington to this god-forsaken outpost. Certainly not someone like you. You came sailing into the residence like a Hollywood star, dressed in golden silk, but with your face black and blue as though you had just been beaten up. And you performed throughout the entire evening as though nothing was amiss."

"I guess I gave my boss, Bill Hart, and his wife Celeste quite a scare when they met me at the airport that afternoon. They didn't think I would want to go to the reception, but I insisted. After all, as they say in Hollywood, you can't let your public down. Hart had been waiting six months for Washington to send him help. I had to show up."

"I don't know about that. Anyone else would have asked to be taken immediately to a doctor."

"Really? I could still walk, and besides I had already seen a doctor in Cairo."

"Why did you come that way, via the back door, as they say?"

"Well, I figured that if I was to be stuck here for two years I might as well see as much of the world as I could instead of coming directly to Leopoldville from Brussels with only one stopover in Timbuktu. I had never seen Athens, or Cairo, or the Sahara. And then I wanted to fly over the whole country in a bush plane. See it all before settling in. But it was a *mistake*," I groaned, continuing to message the blood clot in my cheek. "From the very beginning. And by the time I got to Stanleyville I was convinced that someone up there," I rolled my eyes heavenward, "was trying to tell me something."

"What do you mean?"

"First of all Washington wrote the wrong departure time on my ticket for New York to Brussels, so I missed that flight—and thus the connecting one to Athens. In Athens the flight to Cairo left without me. It was only as they were about to take off, and were all the way down the runway, that they discovered I was missing and turned back to pick me up. Then came Cairo, the accident, but I was still on time for the plane to Stanleyville. Yet when I arrived in Stanleyville, they said I had no reservations for Leopoldville. They didn't know who I was, and Customs refused to recognize my diplomatic passport. Had never seen one there before."

"I guess not. All diplomats come in through Leopoldville."

"But they solved the problem, though, by issuing me an immigrant's card!"

"You mean you got an I.D. card just like that? People spend

months, even years, in Brussels trying to get one. I'd hold onto it, if I were you. It might come in handy some day."

"What for? I'm not going to stay here."

"You never know. Do you want to talk about the accident?"

I waited a minute before replying. Then took a deep breath and said, "All right. If you wish. I remember it as one would a nightmare. Like it never really happened. But every time I look in the mirror I know it did. It was late at night, you see. Around 2 a.m. and we were returning from a party at a villa outside Cairo. I had just arrived in Egypt and was exhausted. I asked to be taken back to my hotel and accepted a ride in a Volkswagen with people I had never met before. The driver was going fast, probably eighty miles an hour, down this broad empty boulevard on the outskirts of Cairo when suddenly, turning a corner, he came face to face with a horse-drawn wagon loaded with telephone poles. He swerved to the left to avoid it. The car shook violently, and, oh, I shall never forget how the tires screamed as we went off the road on two wheels, over the curb and headed straight for a towering stone wall. It came at me like an express train until it was only inches from my face. And I was in the back seat, too. But just before we smashed into it, the driver managed to swerve to the right. The car turned completely over and over and over and over. Five times. We bounced like a ball across that boulevard before finally coming to a halt on the other side at the foot of another stone wall. We landed right side up, but without tires, wheels or doors. The roof had been transformed into a piece of corrugated metal. I was able to climb out, but the others . . ."

"What happened to them?"

"I was later told that the driver and his girlfriend died. And the fellow in the back seat with me—we held onto each other— had every bone in his body broken on his right side where he took a hit each time we rolled over, while I escaped with only a concussion and bruises on my left side, where I took the hits. The Egyptian doctor who took care of me said I must have bones of rubber. Hah!"

I got up and began to walk away from Claude, legs weak. I

could still see that stone wall in Cairo before my face, feel myself rolling over and over, hear myself praying, guts paralyzed with fear, *"No, dear God, please not again."*

Then I saw the crocodiles. I had never seen a crocodile before. Alligators, yes. But not crocodiles. I never imagined that any living creature on this earth could be so ugly. Huge primeval monsters they were. Mini dinosaurs. Fat and slimy—sliding in and out of the mud and ooze of their habitat, half-hiding among the rocks of the zoo's pool. They filled me with disgust. And fear. And also awe. As I watched them, they watched me. Eyes wide open, staring, insolent, cunning, and wise with the craftiness of milleniums of existence. Eyes that looked right through me. Sizing me up. I could be their next meal. I was the prey. They, the hunters. I, the hunted.

"*My God,*" I shivered. "How awful they are!"

"Would you like to hunt them?" Claude asked ever so casually.

I was astonished. "Well," I hesitated. Then, with a gesture indicating the rest of the animals in the zoo, said, "I'd never want to kill any of *them.* But those, yes!" I exclaimed, pointing to the crocodiles.

"Well, then, we'll go."

"Are you serious?"

"Of course. Did you know that apart from disease the crocodile is the cause of more deaths among the Congolese than anything else? It's the one animal you don't need a license to kill. And one of my clerks goes crocodile hunting every Saturday night he can get away."

"Night?"

"Sure. During the day it's almost impossible to see them, so well do they camouflage themselves along the banks of the river. And, besides, they can see you during the day, but during the night, it's their time to hunt. In the river. We go after them in a pirogue and you blind them with a light. Their eyes gleam red in the glare, and it's between those eyes that you must shoot. It's the only place where one bullet can instantly kill, of course."

"Of course."

"Yes," he said, then frowned and looked away, as though he was having second thoughts. "I'll talk to him about it," he mumbled. Turning back to me he added, speaking cautiously, "and then call you. First you must see him. He wouldn't take you if he didn't know you. And who you are. There are things you should know. It's very risky. He's never taken any woman with him before. In his pirogue, I mean. Oh, sure, he's taken a few Belgian women now and then just for the ride." He made a gesture with his well-kept bank manager's hands, dismissing this information as being of little importance, and continued, "For company. However, he always leaves them behind in the village. But maybe an American woman . . . . You're different."

"I'm not sure that's a compliment," I laughed.

He looked into my eyes. "It is." Then, "You're sure you want to go?"

"I don't know, but I guess, as they say, 'when in Rome . . . do as the Romans.' So when one is in the Congo, what does one do? One hunts, I suppose."

What I feared most upon leaving Washington was the boredom I would have to endure during my two years in the Congo. My deadly enemy, I believed, would not be the heat, the threat of malaria, the jungle, or even crocodiles, but ennui. What I dreaded most was finding myself lost in loneliness.

"I couldn't believe it," I told Claude, "when I was actually assigned here. Though I should have suspected something very unusual when that French professor kept following me around during the Foreign Service training. Waiting for me outside every classroom to get some lessons in. Taking up every lunch period. Inviting me out for dinner every night. I knew they weren't grooming me for Paris. That's the ultimate. The last post for senior officers after years of service in French-speaking countries. But I thought perhaps Marseilles. Maybe even Saigon. And when I was called into the African personnel office, I thought it had to be some place in North Africa, say, Casablanca, Rabat, Algiers. But when the Director told me, 'It's Leopoldville,' I was so stunned I couldn't speak. I had just seen *Heart of Darkness* the night before on TV! I looked at the map of Africa on the wall behind her. She asked, 'Do you know where that is?' I managed to mumble, 'yes. The Belgian Congo.' Then she proceeded to present me with a list of recommended reading on the subject. Top of the list of books was *My Life Among The Pygmies* by some woman called Putnam, I believe. Imagine! *Me* from New York! Hollywood! *My Life Among The Pygmies!* And then there was something called *Bring 'Em Back Alive* by Frank Buck."

Claude laughed.

"Or *Explorations in Africa* by Dr. Livingston and Henry Morton Stanley. You know, 'Dr. Livingston, I presume?' Honestly, I was scared and the woman saw that. She knew that I knew that I couldn't refuse to accept my first post. However, she told me, if I was absolutely determined not to go she could offer me a post in Khartoum in the middle of the Sahara. I told her I'd think about it and immediately raced out of the building and down the street to a public telephone. I didn't dare call from the State Department building. There, on the corner of Pennsylvania Avenue, I called my friend, Monsieur de Kémoularia in the Secretary General's office at the United Nations. 'What do I do?' I asked. 'It's either Leopoldville or Khartoum!' He didn't hesitate. 'For God's sake take Leopoldville,' he told me. 'The only thing in Khartoum is one zinc palm and that's in front of the British Embassy.'"

"That's right," Claude agreed, a cynical smile appearing on the edges of his slender lips. "This might be known as the green hell, the green abyss, but it's better than the Sahara. And, yes, here one hunts. Only I wouldn't mention it at the consulate, if I were you. They might not let you go. It's a dangerous business, I tell you."

"I do what I want in my leisure time."

He chuckled.

"By the way," I asked, "what's a zinc palm?"

"A palm tree with a wide band of zinc around the bottom of it so rats can't climb up and get the fruit on top." Then he looked down at me, eyebrows arched. "I hope you don't mind blood," he said. "By the time we're finished, you'll be wading in it. Ankle deep."

"Why?"

"What do you think?"

"You mean you keep them in the boat?"

"Of course. We certainly couldn't drag them alongside. Other crocodiles would finish them off within minutes. They are the meanest animals alive. They even eat their own. Can you shoot?"

"Well, I—"

"No matter. If need be, you can use my pistol. While Henri— my clerk's name is Henri—and I are dragging them in, sometimes you might have to use the pistol between the eyes to finish them off."

"*I would?*"

"Certainly. It's a very serious business. And we all have to work together. Henri, you, I, and his two men. *Teamwork*." He was enjoying himself. "I'll bring an extra hunting knife for you, too."

"How many does your clerk catch in a night?"

"Sometimes ten, fifteen. Sometimes only a couple. He's caught almost all around here. We'll probably have to go up the Congo about sixty miles."

"He must have an awfully big boat."

"No. Just a native pirogue, really, but with an outboard motor."

As we headed back toward his MG I asked, "After your clerk's got them? What does he do with them, right there beside the river?"

"Skins them, of course. Then sends the hides to an outfit in your country in the state of New Jersey called Baron Brothers. Gets between 1,500 and 3,000 Belgian francs a skin, depending on the size."

"That would be between $30 and $60. Is that all?"

"It's better than what he used to get. He used to sell them to Bata here. That's the big shoe and handbag manufacturer in Belgium. They were only giving him 400 francs a skin. $8 to $10! But by mistake one day he got a letter from Baron Brothers, which was meant for Bata and found out what they were selling them to Baron's for. So from then on he sent them to Baron's direct. And as for the meat, he sells or gives it to the natives. Depending on the tribe. Some will never touch it, you know. They fear the crocodile more than anything else. It's the one animal most tribes won't hunt. Some consider it an evil god. Some think of them as their ancestors. And for them, it's like eating their own flesh when the crocodile has eaten members of their family before it was killed. Henri once had a houseboy whose name, in Lingala, meant 'crocodile,' and every time he saw Henri eating the meat he got sick because it was as though Henri was eating him."

As we sped away, driving very fast again, he looked over at me and abruptly asked, "You can swim, can't you?"

"Well, yes. But—"

"Don't worry." He drove on. "You probably won't have to. However, it's just as well that you know how."

"Yes. Of course," I mumbled, now alarmed, wondering what I was getting myself into. I had seen the powerful Congo when flying low over its entire navigable length all the way from Stanleyville to Leopoldville. It was the color of muddy milk as it snaked its broad, silent and mysterious way through the jungle. The bush pilot had told me, "We must follow the river. It's our only navigation instrument. There is no radio contact between Leopoldville and Stanleyville." I had felt an immediate attraction to the Congo's overwhelming force, just as iron is irresistibly attracted to a magnet. But it was not something I would want to find myself swimming in.

Claude glanced at me again, his large black eyes narrowing. Then he threw his head back and suddenly laughed out loud as he continued to speed recklessly down the broad Boulevard Albert.

"Slow down!" I finally screamed. He glanced sideways, annoyed. "I mean it!" I cried out. That wall in Cairo was looming up in front of my face again, and I could feel the car about to turn over.

"And you want to hunt crocodiles?"

"*That's different.* I've never been killed by a crocodile. Yet!"

"Sorry," he said. And he slowed down, almost to a crawl, as we continued on Boulevard Albert toward my hotel. This modern four-lane highway ran through the center of Leopoldville, and with its spacious island of flowering hibiscus and arching neon street lights, it seemed as out of place in this part of the world as Lincoln's log cabin would be in the middle of Times Square.

At the doorway of the Regina I told him, "I'll bring all the food."

It was the only contribution to the proposed expedition I could think of making. "By the time we go I should have my apartment and can make us some tasty things."

"Good. But I can't promise anything. It all depends on Henri. What he thinks of you. Like I said, it's dangerous. But if he agrees to take you, I'll go along." He squeezed my hand and suddenly very serious, his eyes entreating, added, "I'd like that."

As he sped off, once more driving very fast, he called out, "What we'll need mostly is cognac!"

# 2.

## HENRI

O N THE WAY to Henri's place for my "interview," I asked Claude, "Is he married?"

"Yes . . .," he replied, thoughtfully, as though he wasn't quite so sure. "But his wife got fed up with the crocodiles and went back to Belgium. He's just crazy with them. Had them all over the house. In the kitchen. One in the bathtub. It was just too much for her. She tried going with him several times, but, *you know*," he said with that peculiar gesture of his wrist that had now become familiar to me, as though he was brushing away an annoying insect, "he went every weekend, and that's too much for any woman." And then he laughed, making a brief, high-pitched sound that left me feeling vaguely uncomfortable.

"Yes, well," I agreed as I followed Claude up the outside staircase of a two-story apartment building thinking of people I have known who no longer love. Or who are no longer loved and find satisfaction in other things. But *crocodiles*?

When we reached the top of the stairs, Claude paused, looking over the three-building complex and explained, "This is where we house the bank employees. But I, being the manager, get to live on the other side of Leopoldville, away from all of them. *Thank God.* Just imagine what it's like living with the people you work with all day! And all the screaming babies! It's bad enough on one's nerves just being in the Congo, but to have to live like this too . . . . " He shuddered and opened Henri's door, walking right into his apartment without knocking.

The living-dining room combination was crowded with dark, massive, wooden furniture, the chairs and couch upholstered with plastic material, and all badly lit from above with a single weak ceiling light fixture. "Typical Company housing," murmured Claude, glancing over the room. "And furniture. They make the pieces big and sturdy. To last. Ugh. So ugly."

A lonely place setting had been left by Henri's houseboy at the far end of the long, otherwise empty, dining table. It consisted of a napkin covering a dinner plate, flatware, and a water glass turned upside down.

A man's voice called out from another room that he wasn't ready, so Claude and I sat down to wait—I on the couch and Claude on the matching plastic-covered armchair. Among the things scattered on the cluttered coffee table were some bullets, a half bottle of whiskey, and a graceful earthen jug full of more bullets.

To my right stood something that looked like a coat rack hung with various-sized guns, a stuffed buffalo head, and an old clarinet. Then I saw the crocodile on the floor by my feet. Claude picked it up and handed it to me. It was stuffed but amazingly lifelike. A baby crocodile with a graceful tail—too young to be ugly.

While I fingered it, albeit gingerly, Claude began to explain, "It's the skin hunters are after. And the skin has to be shipped, usually by airfreight, rolled up in salt. Everything except the armored back can be used for leather."

"Everything?"

"Including the arms and feet, but it's the underbelly skin

that is preferred and crocodiles of at least two meters are the most worthwhile. Any larger and the skin becomes tough. Preparing the skins is a delicate process, and can't be done in the Congo. Henri immediately rolls up the skins in salt, packs them in a crate, and ships them as quickly as he can. They are good for perhaps three months like that. And when he makes a big catch, he has a Yugoslav do it for him because he doesn't have the time. He and this Slav are the only really professional crocodile hunters in the Congo. But the Slav is in the hospital now."

We continued to wait in silence for the man in the other room. Pictures of crocodiles of all sizes covered the walls. When I got up to examine them closely, Claude told me, "You probably don't realize that there are two types of crocodiles in the Congo. One is the man-eater. His jaw is squared-off at the end. The other is considered a fish-eater only, but I wouldn't count on it. His jaw comes more to a point at the end. It's called a gavial and never attains the same size as a man-eater. For that reason Henri prefers to search out the man-eaters, and they are getting scarce right around here. One has to go farther into the interior for a really good night's haul. They don't like all the traffic on the river now, and besides Henri has shot most of them. Sometimes the government pays him to go after some really troublesome ones. Rogue hippos, too. Outcasts from the herd, who get mean."

"He sounds formidable."

"He is. No one else around here but Henri dares to do these things. Just last month he was sent out to shoot a rogue hippo that would lie in wait for passengers crossing a river in the Kasai and, when the ferry got to the middle, he would come up under it and turn it over. Did you know that a hippo can tear you to pieces just as easily as a crocodile?"

"I thought they were vegetarians."

"Not when they're mad, they're not."

The crocodile hunter continued to keep us waiting, and there was no sound of movement coming from the adjacent room. For a moment I wondered if he was listening to our conversation.

"Did you know that there haven't been crocodiles in the Nile for at least fifty years?" Claude continued. "You have heard of the famous Nile crocodile, yes?"

I nodded.

"Well, they have been finished for a long time. Right now the bulk of the crocodile market is supplied from South America and with the relatively harmless type found in India. Oh, there are a lot of amateurs," he continued, glancing at Henri's guns hanging on the coat rack at his elbow, "but now that this Slav is out of commission, Henri is really the only professional crocodile hunter I know of around here. It's too dangerous. And he doesn't make much profit. Many times he spends much more than he makes in petrol and ammunition. And he has to pay his boys, too."

It was then that Henri made his entrance. I rose and smiled warmly, but he seemed preoccupied as he briefly acknowledged my handshake, hardly glancing at me through his dark, round, steel-rimmed glasses and not looking at all at Claude. His eyes, his thoughts, his entire spirit appeared to be far, far away from his gloomy Leopoldville living room and his guests standing there.

"We'll go over to Brazzaville for dinner," he announced, striding past us, out the door and down the steps to his jeep. We followed. He was as tall as Claude, the same age, but much more solidly built, and his skin matched the color of his khaki shorts. "We'll take my motor boat."

But I hesitated before climbing into his jeep. "Can't we just eat somewhere around here?" I wondered. Yves Quero, my French assistant in the consulate, lived in Brazzaville and had warned me never to cross the Congo at night. The ferries stopped at sundown, which was why he was never able to stay at the consulate after dark for receptions, evening film showings, or any other U.S. Information Service event. He left promptly every afternoon at 4:30 p.m. in time to catch the last ferry. "It's too dangerous to cross in a small boat," he had told me. "Its motor could get snarled in the thousands of island masses of water lilies that clog the river, despite the swift current. With one's motor out of commission, powerless, one could be swept into the rapids that lie just below

Leopoldville. And no boat has ever survived these rapids. Three hundred kilometers of them—all the way to the Atlantic—where the Congo finally empties itself, roiling and boiling, into the sea.

"Even the Queen Mary," Yves had cautioned me, "would be chopped to kindling wood."

Henri turned to face me, frowning. "I mean, surely," I asked once again, "there must be some place you would like to go on this side of the river?"

"No. The best restaurant on either side is an Indo-Chinese one, and it's over there. That's where we'll go."

Still I hesitated, looking at Claude for help. But he looked away. "What's the matter?" Henri asked mildly, "Don't you trust me?"

"Yes, of course, but . . . . " I had to think fast. "But Brazzaville is in a different country. I don't have my passport with me."

"You don't need a passport. Customs is closed at night, anyway. I know how to sneak in."

"All right," I agreed thinking that if I refused to go to Brazzaville, Henri would probably not take me on the hunt. This was my test.

Henri climbed aboard and reached for my hand to help me aboard as well. His grip was firm. As I went I only hoped Bill Hart, my supervisor at the consulate, would never find out. A member of the diplomatic corps sneaking into another country without a passport? Crossing the second largest river in the world at night, and at its most dangerous point, when she had been warned not to? Recklessly putting her life in danger just to go to a restaurant after all the money the State Department had spent on her training?

Henri's speedboat was small but sturdy. After he had started the motor, and as we pulled away from the dock, I looked back at the shoreline where I could make out a group of men on the porch of the yacht club on the hill above, playing cards in the dim light of a kerosene lamp. Otherwise, all was quiet and deserted. The men on the porch did not look up from their game as we sailed away from the dark land.

After we had reached the main channel, Henri drove the speedboat with one hand, standing up, and held a powerful searchlight in the other, playing it over the clumps of water lily plants ahead. We dodged in and out of their way, zigzagging back and forth. Twice the motor showed signs of clogging, but Henri was able to give it enough extra power to free it from the clutches of the roots of these insidious plants. Twice the motor stopped altogether. When this happened, Henri pulled it up out of the water, whipped out the big knife he carried in a leather sheath around his waist, and swiftly cut away the roots choking the blades. I held my breath, feeling the powerless boat quickly drifting in the swiftly flowing current toward the nearby rapids, whose roar could be distinctly heard. I remembered Quero telling me how many boats venturing too close to the edge of these rapids had been lost. He told me about one newspaperman he knew who was having trouble with his motor and got too close. A nearby native pirogue tried to warn him, but he, sure he could get the motor going in time, waved it away. "Too late," Quero had said. "He was lost in a flash."

The third time the motor stopped Claude rose to his feet shouting to me, "These damn weeds! The curse of some well-meaning missionary who brought the seeds from Brazil. But here they took root like cancers out of control and he's been dammed ever since. Probably more often than the weather or the mosquitoes."

Once again Henri managed to free the clogged propeller, and Claude settled back down on his seat. I couldn't see his face, but I suspected he was becoming as nervous as I.

"We'll be okay, Elise. We'll make it, don't you worry. Won't we, Henri?" But Henri didn't answer. He continued standing, staring over our heads at the treacherous waters, his strong naked legs spread wide apart, one hand on the tiller, the other holding his searchlight, on guard for the next mass of killer weeds heading in our direction.

We finally arrived on the Brazzaville side of the river twenty minutes after having left Leopoldville. All was silent at the

Customs shed that bustled during daylight hours with workers coming across to jobs in the more affluent Belgian colony. We ducked under the barrier thrown across the quay road and started walking along the dark, dirt road toward the lights of the capital of the French colony.

Henri's English was not as good as Claude's, so we spoke a combination of my bad French and his bad English as we walked together. Or rather I asked questions, and he answered as laconically as was possible and still be polite.

"Yes. It took me a whole year before I was able to shoot them right. Then the second year I got about fifty. The third, one hundred-fifty. This year, I want five hundred."

"That's quite a few, you know," commented Claude, "for now-and-then weekend hunting."

We walked for fifteen minutes before we found Henri's restaurant. It had a bar on the ground floor facing the main street of the sleepy, rundown colonial town. A pretty Oriental girl was sitting primly on one stool. I was surprised to find her there, being the first I had so far seen. Her companion, the only other client in the place, was a haggard looking, unshaven French *colon*. The girl's eyes followed me, a puzzled expression on her face, as I walked up the stairs behind Henri to the restaurant above.

Henri introduced me to the manager. "From Saigon," he explained. "The girl downstairs is his daughter. They had the best restaurant there when it was still a French colony. Had to run, of course, when they pulled out."

He greeted Henri enthusiastically. We were his only clients in a restaurant that covered the entire top floor of half a block of stores. "Things were different," he apologized, "before the trouble."

"Trouble?" I asked Claude.

"Yes. The riots. They want independence. Hah!"

Henri looked at him hard. "They'll get it, though. But it will come from across the river. It will come first to the Belgian Congo."

"You think so?"

"I know so."

"But not now," Claude told him. "Not within the next ten years, at least."

"Sooner than that. Much, much sooner than you and Brussels think."

Claude's mouth tightened. "Well, I certainly hope I won't be around to witness it. It will be a disaster. Chaos."

Henri shrugged and strode to a table out on the little balcony overlooking the main street below, empty of all traffic and pedestrians.

The manager immediately brought a bottle of Pernod, which we drank with ice and water. There was no menu, and Henri ordered for all of us. First, we had a kind of spinach soup, made from the leaves of the manioc plant. Then came broiled fish, resembling trout. "*Capitaine,*" Henri said, "from the river."

"Delicious," said I, pleased to learn that the Congo River produced something else besides crocodiles, hippos, and killer water lilies.

He nodded and again fell silent, bent over his food. The crew cut that he wore only called attention to the unusual size of his squared-off head. He was from the eastern part of Belgium. Flemish country; whereas Claude was a Walloon, from the French part of Belgium.

I attempted to engage him in conversation. "My assistant, who lives in Brazzaville, told me a story," I began, "about a U.S. Air Force officer who was stationed here and was drowned by a crocodile."

"*Oui?*" He appeared only mildly interested.

"Yes," I continued. "He liked to go swimming in one of the sandy-beached inlets along the shore, though he was warned many times about the dangers of stray crocodiles. But after a year of never having seen one, he swam about with his family every Sunday without fear. The last time he went, though, he went too far out. His little daughter saw a crocodile approaching and called to him from the beach. But he didn't pay any attention, either thinking it was a joke, or not understanding. When he did see it, it was too late. The crocodile caught him by the leg and carried him under. They say it buried him somewhere among the rocks or under a sandbank and would come back to eat him later. Is that true?"

Henri looked up and sighed, a bored expression on his face. "They never eat fresh meat," he said. "They stash it in their dens and leave it there to rot. Then come back to eat it later. Bodies so lost are never found."

Claude offered, "A crocodile got a Frenchman once up the river, but there happened to be a little air hole where he was buried, so he escaped after his jailer left. And lived."

"What a thing to live through!" I shuddered. "So, actually, Henri, they kill you by drowning?"

"That's right. And in the process, of course, they can bite off your leg. Or your arm."

Another delicacy arrived at our table: chopped meat wrapped up in leaves, which Henri dipped into a sweet sauce first and then into a hot one. I followed his example but gasped after tasting the hot sauce, reaching quickly for the water glass. "It's *pili-pili*," said Henri. "You'll get used to it if you stay here long enough. It's the native equivalent to your Louisiana hot peppers, only ten times stronger."

The men went back to eating in silence while I recovered from my first dose of pili-pili. Suddenly Henri lifted up his head and looked at Claude. "I think we'll take her up the Kwango. The Congo wouldn't be very exciting."

My heart flipped. Then stood still. "Where's the Kwango?" I asked in a weak voice.

He smiled at me for the first time, his severe features dissolving like melting wax and becoming surprisingly soft, almost gentle. His eyes smiled at me as well. I had passed my test.

"In the Kasai," he replied. "East of here. We will have to go in my jeep for about 175 kilometers, but I think it will be worthwhile. You will be able to hear much there at night. Elephants. Even a lion's roar once or twice. And, of course, the monkeys, the baboons . . . . I have a pirogue there."

"*Wonderful.*"

"Of course," he warned, "in the pirogue you will have to remain very still."

"Of course."

The manager served the entrée: curried buffalo meat with condiments of pickled papaya and sunflower seeds mashed together with sardines. We drank a dry white Portuguese wine.

As Henri reached for the bottle, his sleeve pulled back. His wrist and forearm were badly mangled. "Yes," he replied to my unspoken question. "One of them did get me. I had shot it, jumped into the water to get it before it sank, but it was not dead. It clamped onto my arm." To demonstrate, he came down with his left arm, vice-like, onto his mangled right with such force it made me jump in my seat. Both of us stared at it for a long moment before he pulled his sleeve back down.

"My boy in the boat tried to shoot," he continued, "but the gun jammed and it was some minutes before he could finally kill it . . . . That put me in the hospital for a while," he added with a note of wonder in his voice as though he still couldn't understand how or why it had happened.

"Didn't that make you want to stop?"

His face clouded over and he replied in a harsh voice, "No. *It made me hate them all the more.*"

Claude asked, "How were the hippos Saturday?"

"Hundreds of them," Henri replied with some disgust. "It was quite a work trying to keep away. But I don't think there will be many next Saturday. We had the full moon then, remember? And no matter, anyway. The boys are pretty good."

He smiled again as he looked at me saying, "We went over one—way up and way down—like going over a wave and the boy just lifted the motor high in the air."

"They will only attack if they are hurt," Claude explained.

"There's something else that happened, too," he told me. "Something I swear has never happened before, and certainly will never happen again. Even the natives told me they had never heard of anything like it happening before."

"What?"

"A crocodile jumped right into the boat! He got my boy's foot, slashed around, and then went after me. We had to jump overboard immediately. Had no time to shoot it. Then we spent one hour pushing the boat to the shore. Finally, we were able to make a lasso and get it out of the boat that way."

"And your boy?" I asked. "Good grief! What happened to him?"

"Oh. He only lost his shoe."

Claude laughed and in the next breath announced, "Elise says she will bring the food."

"Good," Henri sighed, looking away, perhaps still thinking of the crocodile that jumped into his pirogue. Then he added, returning his gaze to mine, "And you shouldn't forget a first-aid kit for yourself, and rubber shoes, and a change of clothing."

"Yes. And what about breakfast? Shall I bring a frying pan and some bacon and eggs?"

He laughed. "That should be interesting. But forget the eggs. I'll find some crocodile eggs."

"Then for lunch?"

"We'll have crocodile stew. Just remember to bring two cans of tomato paste and an onion. The boys will have the pili-pili. And, oh, make sure you take your anti-malaria pill. Once, in the beginning, when I hunted alone, a hippo overturned my pirogue. It got away from me. I had to stay on a sandbank for two days before I was rescued, all the while eaten alive by mosquitoes. Came down with an attack of malaria, of course. But that time it was really bad. Put me in the hospital. For *three* months."

"Don't worry," I promised. "I won't forget."

The wine I had drunk gave me courage as I walked back between these two strange men along the dark road carved out of the jungle toward the beach and Henri's motorboat. The branches of great trees on either side overhung the path, shutting out all light, including the waning moon and the stars.

"Why, Henri," I dared to ask, "do you hate them so much?"

He didn't hesitate. "It's those red eyes," he growled, making a harsh sound as though spitting something bitter out of his mouth. "It's those red eyes."

# 3.

## CLAUDE'S STORY

"IT'S BEST YOU take an apartment here, Elise, within the complex," Bill Hart advised, leaning back in his chair. He was a soft-spoken man in his mid-forties, not yet graying, and had the easy-going manner of a "southern gentleman." Indeed, he had come to the Foreign Service from a southern university, where he had been a professor of linguistics. He spoke five languages fluently and had the off-handed mannerisms of the enduring professor, as well as the perpetually wrinkled suit and loosely knotted tie. But it didn't take me long to realize that his gentle voice and kind eyes all belied a superior sophistication learned from years in the Service dealing with foreign government officials and members of the press, representing many diverse cultures and disparate ways of thinking. He was a superb diplomat.

"Why?"

He leaned forward, elbows resting on his desk, and his dark brown eyes looked into mine, as he twiddled a pencil between his fingers. "Well . . . . "

He dropped his pencil and tossed back his oversized head. "First reason: the January riots. They could flare up again at any time. Security reports there is still a great deal of unrest in the African *cité*. You weren't here for the riots. I can tell you it wasn't a pretty sight."

"But I'm not Belgian. The Congolese have nothing against us."

Bill chuckled. "You are white. That's all they can see."

I glanced away from his steady gaze, looking past him out the window at the block of two-story apartment buildings in the rear of the consulate. This was where most of the single members of the consulate lived. "Look, Bill, I couldn't live there. Why, it would be like living in a dormitory. You must understand I'm not twenty-one."

He chuckled again. "Twenty-five. I know."

I ignored his sarcasm. "I'm used to being independent. To coming and going as I please, without everyone and his cousin knowing what I am doing. Who I am seeing."

He nodded again. "All I know is that this is your first post and you're my responsibility. You're pretty, single, and obviously have your own reasons for joining the U. S. Information Service other than the fact that you need a job. I suspect that you haven't come to us just because you want to travel and see the world. However, that's none of my business. Washington sent you because of your unusual background in public relations."

"And the fact that I can speak French."

"Yes. That, too. Look, Washington knows they are taking a chance. They don't expect you to last. But as long as you're here, it's my job to see that you do your job without me or Washington having to worry about your safety."

"Bill," I continued to cajole, staring directly into his eyes, "do you know Raymond Fourrier's place? Out on the Grand Cornice?"

"What about it?"

"It's so beautiful. I was out there last night for dinner, and I fell in love with it. Great tropical gardens falling away from a Swiss chalet into the Congo rapids just beyond. You can barely see them, but, oh, you can hear them! Fourrier's returning to Switzerland next week for four months, and he said I could have his place while he's gone."

"Out of the question."

"But why? It's free."

"Nothing is free."

"But it is! And furnished, too. Why not?"

*"Because it's too far away."*

"I see . . . . But I won't stay in one of those." I pointed to the consulate's apartment complex. "I must be by the river. Now that I have seen it, I must at least have a view of it. I didn't come all the way here not to know it. Feel it. After all, what else is there here?"

He leaned forward again and sighed deeply. "I'll tell you what. There's a new high-rise apartment house not too far from here. Probably five minutes by car. Right on the river. Built by Unilever for their executives and other high-ranking employees, but they do rent out some apartments to qualified tenants when one comes free. I hear there's one available now."

"Good."

He rose to his feet. "Let's go take a look."

It was on the sixth floor. One entire wall of the spacious living room was made of glass, and as I walked in I could see the mighty Congo sparkling in the sunshine below. What's more, one of these glass windows contained a door leading to a balcony overlooking the river. I stepped out and was greeted by a sapphire-blue sky, and mountainous, low-lying, luminously white African clouds were scattered about as lavishly as whipped cream on a wedding cake. Bill followed me out onto the balcony. "It's perfect," I agreed.

He said nothing. Thinking. Admiring the view as well.

"But I have no furniture."

"Don't worry. We've got some in storage you can borrow as long as you're here. Things other people have left behind. There's a bed, a couch, a couple of chairs. You can take one of the tables from the library to use as a dining room table."

"Thank you. I'll take anything."

"Good."

He continued to stare down at the river. In the silence of the midday heat all that could be heard was the distant roar of the rapids below the city. He shook his head. "You have to be careful here. So many have lost their heads. I don't know . . . . The Congo *does* something to you. Looking at this river reminds me of something I saw when I first arrived. Something extraordinary. I was standing on the hill overlooking the port and watching the steamboats put in with all their barges, when suddenly the biggest one of them all, the newest one, broke away. After his barges had been unhooked and his passengers and crew had disembarked, its captain took it out to the middle of the river and then headed, full steam, for the rapids. And over he went, whistle blowing so hard all of Leopoldville could hear."

I drew in my breath. *"What a way to go.* Do you know why?"

"Well, it seems that he had made that run Leopoldville-Stanleyville for years. Ten days up, ten days back. Three thousand miles in all through the jungle. His wife usually accompanied him, as many Flemish women do. He was Flemish, of course. All the river boat captains here are. But one day she got fed up, left him, went back to Belgium. After six months of slowly going crazy, I guess, he just lost it altogether."

The next day Hart arranged for my purchase of a German-made Ford—a 1954 Tunis—and by the end of the week I was installed in my new domain, together with a houseboy. When I protested that I didn't need one, Bill replied, "Oh, yes, you will. You will have no time for housework, washing, or ironing, or even shopping. In your job you will be expected to attend a reception of some kind or another every night of the week. You see, stores around here, including the banks, are closed when we don't work and open when we do. Despite all reason, we have to keep the same hours as Washington. You'll need a houseboy to do your shopping for you, if nothing else. But don't worry. You won't see much of this houseboy. He gets you up for breakfast at six. Then you tell him what you want him to do. What you want washed, what errands you want him to run, what you want him to set out for your supper, in case you're eating in. He leaves at noon, unless you are entertaining that evening. And it won't cost you. Since Leopoldville is considered a hardship post, part of your twenty-five percent salary bonus goes for that."

"A reception every night?"

"Just about. Though it's only a Belgian colony, every European nation has a consulate here. Some national figure is always coming or going. And there's always someone's national holiday to celebrate. Then there's the weekly Voice of America film show at the library, which, now that you are here, we shall be starting up again. And I hope you will begin giving English lessons soon as well. They have to be at night, too."

"I'd like that. To whom?"

"A few up-coming Congolese politicos. Approved by the Belgian government, of course."

The houseboy arrangement worked out fine. His name was Jean-Pierre, and he would arrive on bicycle from the African *cité* at 5:30 a.m. to take charge. Short, stocky, and efficient, eager to please, he had bright, intelligent eyes with a broad smile to match his natural sense of youthful humor. The second day he arrived with an old jungle drum, which he said belonged to his family in the Lower Congo. It was made of ebony and covered with the footpad of an elephant. He placed it outside my bedroom door and beat on it to rouse me in the morning, thoroughly pleased with the way I instantly responded to this kind of wake-up call. Thanks to Jean-Pierre, by the time I had showered and dressed, I was able to walk out on my balcony to find my breakfast of either mango, papaya, or passion fruit, toast, coffee, and soft-boiled egg awaiting me as I came face to face with the morning sky and said hello to the Congo below.

The day I moved into my new apartment a dozen of the most beautiful roses I had ever seen arrived saying, "Welcome." Packaged individually, the blossoms were enormous, black-red, the color of dried blood, with the texture of velvet. Yves Quero from my office, who was helping me with my move, was impressed. "They are flown in from Holland, and cost $5 each! The Congo has beautiful roses, too, that come from the Kivu, in the Eastern Highlands, but nothing like *these*."

The card was signed, "Claude."

He called early the next morning. "I must talk to you, Elise. There are some things I must tell you."

He spoke with utmost urgency, with much pain in his voice.

"Of course," I quickly replied. "What about lunch?"

"No. Later. It's going to take some time."

"Well, fine. But I have a reception at seven. Do you want to make it for a drink? Say at five? At my place?"

"I'd rather you came to mine. There are some things I want to show you."

"Fine."

"4:30?"

"Let's say 4:45. I only get out at 4:30."

"All right."

"Take it easy, Claude," I added.

"Sure."

I was as off-handedly gay and distant as I knew how to be when I entered his apartment, not looking forward to any confrontation or confession I suspected he might be preparing to unload on me. And I hoped my attitude would help him change his mind in case he had planned on doing so.

I coldly offered him my hand to shake, instead of my cheek to kiss, as was the custom, and immediately withdrew my hand from his before he could shake it properly.

So I was surprised when he announced, "I'm soon being transferred to our branch in Goma."

"Where's that?"

"In the Kivu. All the way on the other side of the Congo. About as far away from this place as I can get and still be in the same country. It will be for six months, maybe longer. Is there anything you might want to use until I come back?" His hand swept over his apartment. "Some things I don't want to store.

This rug, for instance, would be ruined if I did. There's no air conditioning in the warehouse, and it would only get moldy or eaten by bugs. Would you like to hold it for me?"

I was relieved. This meeting was only about furniture. "Gladly," I replied. "I don't have any rugs." It was a beautiful Persian, rose-red mixed with brilliant blues.

"There's also an older one in the bedroom."

It was not as colorful, but the fading greens and pinks were soft and pleasing to the eye. "All donations gratefully accepted."

"Come into the kitchen. I want you to pick out anything you need." He opened the pantry and cupboards, and I choose several pots, pans, and a few other utensils. "What about these dishes?" he offered. "They're Limoges."

"Oh, no. I couldn't trust my houseboy with them. There's no harm in storing dishes."

"Would you like the washing machine?"

"Well, that's a little extravagant, isn't it? I mean, I'm all alone. There's not much to wash. Besides, I doubt if my houseboy would know how to operate it."

Back in the living room, which was furnished with Grade A Congo furniture made especially for the tropics, Claude put a tape of Russian folk music on his recorder. "Would you like to hold this machine for me as well? It comes with my collection, and the tapes could deteriorate in storage."

"I'd love to. How I miss my music! The only thing I have is a small, portable short-wave radio that runs on flashlight batteries."

He nodded. "I know the kind. They're useful but the batteries tend to leak in this climate."

"I promise to take care of everything very well."

"I'm sure you will. I'll have the bank deliver the stuff to you before I go. Would you like a whiskey?"

"How about some tea? I'll make it now that I know where things are."

I found him sitting out on his balcony, watching the lights of the city begin to appear four stories below among the tall palms and mango trees whose leaves were so dark a green they appeared almost black. There was also a view of the Baptist Mission tennis court, where, it appeared, the couples played by rote in the heat and hazy half-light of the approaching night.

"I love that music," Claude said, listening to the sounds of the melancholy folk songs drifting out of the living room onto the balcony. "In fact, I like everything Russian. I speak it, you know."

"How many languages do you speak?"

"Well, French, of course. Then English, Flemish and Dutch, German, Russian, Spanish, Portuguese, Italian, Swahili, Lingala, and some Kikongo that I picked up while in the Kasai. Twelve. Not unusual for a man like me."

He changed the subject saying, "You must wonder where all these things come from. Why a single man here has a washing machine."

He stared at me intently, waiting for my reply. I looked down at my tea for a moment before confronting his wide-open, blazing black eyes and said, "I know you were married, Claude."

"But do you know what happened?" he demanded, his voice suddenly taking on a harsh note.

"Yes." I hesitated. Then added, my voice low, "I was told your wife was killed in an automobile accident about a year ago. I'm sorry."

He leaned forward in his chair, his face very close to mine. "Who told you *that*?"

"Mrs. de Coster."

"That stupid woman! Why would she ever have said something like that? Did she think she was doing me some kind of a favor? Hah!"

He settled back into his chair. "It's not true."

I waited.

"She committed *suicide*."

"Oh . . . . "

"Right here. In Leopoldville. Two years ago. In one of those apartment houses that belong to the bank. She jumped from the fourth floor."

He sat straight back, stiffly holding the teacup on his knee, lips taut and sometimes twitching in his effort to remain calm. After a few minutes he rose and placed the teacup on the balcony railing, turned to face me and began, "I met her after the war at a dance given by my university. We were both very young, and I was very bitter. If I had been able to join the Party, I'd have been a Communist. I was mad at the world."

"You were in the war? You don't look that old."

"I was in the *maquis*. Not the fighting maquis. Just the hiding maquis. A group of us kids took to the hills when we were old enough to be sent to labor camps in Germany. We raided and stole and sabotaged whenever we could. My father spent five years in a concentration camp. I'll never be able to forget what he looked like when he came back. Just a skeleton. And my older brother was killed . . . ."

"I don't know how we all managed to stay alive—those other fellows and me. That was when I learned what fear was. The hot, paralyzing kind each time I had a run-in with a German sentry. And I never got used to it. Each time was worse than the last . . . ."

"Only one of us got it. Just before the liberation. But he had gone berserk by then and would take unnecessary risks all the time."

Quietly, I told him, "What always amazes me are not those who lost their sanity, but the number who managed to keep it."

"Yes. But how much of it have we kept, I wonder?" He shrugged and quickly added, "It's not important, anyway." Then he went on with his story. "You see, after we met we were engaged right away. But we had to wait three years before we could marry. I was graduated as a lawyer and an apprentice lawyer makes practically nothing. How much would you say?"

"I don't know. $30 a week?"

"Hah! Six dollars a month. Well, I tried it, but it was impossible. That's when I joined the bank. And we got married. The day after the wedding I knew it was a mistake."

He strode abruptly back into the living room and returned with a photo album of wedding pictures. Opened it and thrust the picture of his wedding party into my lap. I looked carefully at the smiling, hopeful figure of his pretty blonde bride. There was a profound sadness, though, in her blue eyes, as though even then she was calling out for help.

But Claude wasn't pointing to his bride. It was the small, raven-haired girl in pink satin with large dark eyes standing next to her and holding a bridesmaid bouquet that he wanted me to look at.

"Then she came into my life. She was her cousin and best friend. Two months after the wedding I knew I was completely and madly in love with her. And she with me. She was married, too . . . . "

He took the album from me, closed it, and sat down again, setting the book carefully on the railing next to his teacup.

"My wife became pregnant the first month," he continued. "I felt the only thing I could do was to tell the cousin I didn't love her. That I was, had been, only playing with her. It was horrible to have to live that kind of lie. And she *believed* me. She still believes to this day that I hate her. *Can you imagine what that's like?*" he begged to know, self-loathing clearly visible in his eyes.

I nodded. I understood. He turned away and continued speaking, staring straight ahead into the tops of the trees beyond. "My wife suspected something. She never said anything, but I knew she knew. We became like strangers who hardly ever spoke to each other . . . . The second baby arrived a year later. After that, there was nothing.

"Everyone—all the relatives—knew about the cousin and me, and they would try to hint to my wife that I was no good and that she should divorce me. They tried in every way to break it up. Little things, you know. It wasn't easy for her. And I . . . . I didn't help either. I realize now that I was always trying to make her feel small, parading my intelligence all over the place. Making her feel stupid. Crushing her. Crushing her personality. Her confidence in herself. You know, making her feel like *that*." He made a gesture with his thumb and forefinger indicating nothingness.

"Well, the bank transferred me to the Congo. At first she

didn't want to go. I left. But a few weeks later she changed her mind and flew down with the children. She hated it immediately. That's when the suicide threats really started."

Once again, he took a deep breath. "She became friends with Henri and his wife. She and Henri were together a great deal. I knew there was nothing between them but rumors began. You haven't been here long enough to know how vicious people can be here. This green hell invades not only the body of the white man but his mind as well. Just wait," he shook his finger at me, warning, "Just you wait. You'll see!"

Claude rose and began to pace the length of the balcony. "Well, anyway," he continued after a few minutes, "this gossip about my wife and Henri upset her very much. All she talked about was suicide. Then she discovered she was pregnant again, and this depressed her even more. Honestly, I don't know how it happened. Some evil gossip even suggested it might be Henri's, but I don't believe it . . . . "

"Henri is a strange man, isn't he?" I asked, in a vague attempt to change the subject. "Why is he so obsessed with crocodiles? Why did he say it's their red eyes he hates?"

"I don't know. Frankly, I don't know. It could have something to do with what happened to him during the war. He was taken prisoner by the Nazis in the very beginning and sent to a forced labor camp. But he escaped, I believe, and had to be constantly on the run. Finding food at night. Maybe that's it. Most animals' eyes glow red at night when a spotlight is beamed at them. Guard dogs, you know."

I understood, but only vaguely, and said, "Somehow I can't picture a man like him working in a bank."

"Oh, he's not interested in banking! He just wanted to come to the Congo. Anything to get away from Europe."

"I see . . . . "

Claude sat down once more, sighing deeply, and continued with his story. "After my wife learned she was pregnant, she wouldn't do anything . . . ," he murmured, looking down at his hands. Then he suddenly cried out, leaning forward, his eyes pleading for my understanding, saying, "Oh! I *tried*. I really *tried* to get her to go out. Each morning I would write out things for her to do, but when I came home she would still be sitting in the same chair where I had left her in the morning. Then, to make things worse, she received news that her father had died. She had loved him very much. I know now she felt truly lost after that . . . . " His voice cracked.

It was a full minute before he was able to continue. "The day before she died she talked to a Jesuit who was visiting from Brazzaville. He stopped by the bank, and I asked him to see her. He told me that afternoon that I had better get her out of here immediately and back to a psychiatrist in Europe. That night I told her and promised to buy the tickets the next day. And then we had a long talk. The best one we had ever had. She told me all about her family. Her childhood. Some terrible things. You can't imagine. How she hated her Mother! *Eh bien*, we were closer that night than we had ever been in our whole lives, and she seemed happy for the first time."

He smiled ever so sadly, his hands gripping the arms of his chair as he turned towards me. "I came home. at noon the next day to check on her and tell her the plane would be leaving in three days. But I noticed right away that the happiness of the night before had gone. She was the same old way once more."

He stopped, gazing down at the tennis players below, then lifted his eyes to the trees, and finally stared straight ahead at the roofs of the city beyond now enshrined in the pink glow of sunset. When his eyes returned to meet mine he said in a wondering voice, as though still unable to believe what had happened, "I had just stepped out of the elevator, going back to the bank, when I heard a crash in the courtyard. I knew it was she even before I reached her . . . . She never regained consciousness completely. When she did wake up, she said over and over, 'What happened? What happened to me? Tell me, what has happened to me?' She died three hours later."

The Russian folk song had long since played out, and the

only sound in the night was that of tennis balls being hit below. Plop. Plop. Plop. Back and forth. Plop. Plop. Plop.

After a few moments Claude took a deep breath, and a brief, bitter smile settled for a moment on his lips, disappearing as he confessed with wonderment in his voice, "You know, I felt a tremendous relief. A tremendous relief."

"Of course."

He was silent for a while. Plop, plop, plop went the tennis balls. Then he said slowly, softly, "The children were playing in the courtyard. They saw it all."

"Oh . . . ! How *horrible*." My hand flew to my mouth.

"Yes, and I couldn't even go to them right away! The police had to question me. To find out if *I* had killed her."

"My God!"

"It was a good thing she had talked to that Jesuit. He explained and supported my story. And, of course, he arranged for a religious funeral for her. But the hardest thing was explaining to the children. That night I went to them. Mrs. de Coster had taken them. 'Mommy is in heaven. God has taken Mommy away with Him,' I told them . . . .

"You know, the thing I remember about it the most?"

I felt numb and could only shake my head.

"It was later. When I heard my children talking. My little son asked his sister, 'What is heaven? Where is heaven?' And she answered, 'Heaven is a place where, if you go there, you never come back.'"

He got up once more and, gripping the railing, looked out at Leopoldville and then up at the evening sky where the first stars had begun to appear. "Yes. That's what heaven is," he murmured. "I can never seem to forget hearing my little girl say that."

"Where are your children now?"

"Back in Belgium with their grandmother. It's strange, you know, they still haven't forgotten their mother. They still write of her."

"Of course. You haven't seen them since?"

He whirled around and almost shouted, "*How can I?* It's too expensive to bring them here! And *then* what would I do with them? You can't get a nursemaid here. And you certainly couldn't leave them with a houseboy."

"No," I agreed. Then I asked, ever so carefully, "Why have you told me all this, Claude?"

He didn't hesitate. "I had to have someone to talk to. It was getting too much for me. I thought I was going to explode. And when I met you . . . . Well, you seemed to be the only one I've ever met here I could talk to. Who would understand."

He paused, looking at me intently, pleading. There were tears in his eyes. "Understand *me*. That's all." He turned away, mumbling, "Everyone needs to be understood a few times in his life. A few times, at least."

"Yes. I know," I replied, my voice barely audible.

"And you don't hate me?"

"No." I leaned forward and said, almost in a whisper, "We all do the best we can. That's all we can do. And go on doing the best we can."

"But I didn't do the best I could have for her."

"It looks that way to you now. But you thought you were then."

"No. I knew, and not very subconsciously either, that I was killing her."

I rose from my chair. "Look, Claude, she killed *herself*. One thing I've learned in this life is that we are all responsible to ourselves for ourselves."

"Everyone isn't, you know. Isn't responsible. Some just aren't capable of it."

I calmed down. "Yes," I murmured. "You are right. There is no one single truth that applies to us all. We can only hope to snatch at bits and pieces."

By now the sun had completely disappeared, and I began to feel the chill of the night air. I reached out for Claude's hand. It was the hand of a man teetering so close to the edge of despair that he would risk telling his story to someone who was, in reality, almost a complete stranger. I could not help him. The best I could do was to hold his hand.

"It was awful trying to live here afterward," he went on, with my hand now in his. "Just imagine what everyone was thinking of me: a man so bad his wife had to commit suicide. I wanted to leave. To go back to Belgium. But the bank wouldn't let me. They felt it would be better for me to stick it out here. God knows why . . . . "

"Why didn't you quit?"

Once again he hit back hard, withdrawing his hand from mine. "One doesn't quit just like that!" He snapped his fingers. "With two children to support! This isn't the States. Jobs aren't so easy to find. In Belgium when a man is married, he sticks to his job for the rest of his life, whether he likes it or not. When you have children, you don't just get up like *that* and walk away like a carefree bachelor."

"Of course." I rose. "I'll make us some more tea. Don't get up."

When I reappeared on his balcony he was sitting down, leaning forward, with his bent head in his hands. He looked up at me. He had been crying. "You'll be late for your reception."

"It doesn't matter. I'll drop in later. Say I've been delayed. Here, drink your tea."

He drank quickly and when he had finished, he lifted his head high and breathed deeply as though to recharge his lungs. "My life," he moaned, "just one mistake after another. It's like a treadmill. Once you get on you never seem to be able to get off. The music goes on and on and you go round and round. Like a carousel. Round and round. Faster and faster. It never stops."

Then he begged to know with the voice of a desperate man, "Do you think there's any hope that one can jump off?"

He was staring at his right hand. "A fortune teller once said a new life would start for me after forty. I've got eight years to go. I wonder if I'll make it." His gaze returned to mine. "One thing I know, though. I've got to get out of this place."

"You must. Perhaps there's a time for sticking things out, but then there comes the time for running and for running fast. Times when you can't do anything else but run. May I see your music collection? Can you play me something else?"

"Why, yes, of course. Do you like Vivaldi?"

"Lovely."

He rose and disappeared back into the living room. Soon I was listening to the beginning of "The Four Seasons."

When he rejoined me on the balcony he said, "I suppose your reception will be over by now."

"Yes. But it doesn't matter."

"Yes, it does. I'm sorry."

"Don't be foolish. But I'll go now, if you wish."

"Sure."

"Hold on, Claude. Hold on," I urged, taking both his hands in mine and at the same time speaking to him with my eyes. Words were worthless. "Don't be too hard on yourself. I'm beginning to believe that somewhere inside every one of us lies a crippled child, a broken heart. You'll be out of this city soon. Maybe . . . . "

"Yes. Certainly."

I left him then. Quickly.


The following evening I found another dozen roses from Holland on my doorstep. The card read: "Thank you for becoming my friend."

He called later. "Are you ready for the hunt tomorrow? You're still going, aren't you?"

"Of course."

"Henri is looking forward to it. But if you don't want me to go, I won't."

"Of course I do!"

Once reassured, he went over the list of things I was responsible for bringing. "We'll pick you up at 1 p.m. The bank closes at noon."

"*D'accord.*"

Before hanging up he concluded with great feeling, "I'm glad I shall be able to be with you this weekend, Elise. You understand?"

"Yes. I do."

"You are a kind person."

"Don't be silly."
"Yes, you are."
"Okay, then, I am. À *demain*."
"Yes. Until tomorrow."

# 4.

## THE KWANGO

B Y 1:30 P.M. we had left Leopoldville behind and were
well on our way, the three of us squeezed into the front
seat of Henri's open jeep bouncing over rutted, dirt roads, heading
for the Kwango.

Henri drove fast. The winds were strong, the sky overcast
and the hot, humid tropical air felt more oppressive than usual
as we barreled along toward the Kenge-Popokabaka road. Henri
was bareheaded and his brown, crew-cut, sun-bleached hair was
the same color as the sand in the road. In comparison to his
rugged, weatherworn complexion and stolid square-jawed
features, Claude appeared almost feminine. An old-fashioned,
colonial-style pith helmet sat incongruously atop his sleek,
carefully barbered head of black hair.

Strands of my own black hair escaped from under the skimpy
silk scarf I had tied under my chin and flew about my face in the
wind and dust that we kicked up as we sped along the dirt road.
Claude glanced at me, amused. Then he took off his pith helmet

and placed it firmly on my head. It felt good: a fitting touch to the African adventure before me and I smiled up at him gratefully.

About fifteen minutes out of Leopoldville, the dense jungle that surrounded the city gave way to rolling green hills for many miles. The roar of the jeep's powerful motor, and the rush of the wind, made any conversation difficult. Henri seldom turned his intense gaze from the winding road ahead, hanging over the wheel, cradling it in his arms liked a beloved object. As I glanced at him, I saw that he had a thin mustache, which somehow I had failed to notice before, outlining a pair of full, sensual lips. Lips that didn't at all go with his impassive demeanor. After driving for an hour without exchanging a single word with either Claude or me, Henri abruptly stopped in a valley by the side of a swiftly flowing black river. He got out, descended to the bank, and proceeded to wash the sand of the road from his face. I followed.

It was a lovely spot. Massive, fir-green tropical trees crowded together by the riverside, forming a wall of vegetation along the shoreline. Their color, and the shade they provided, gave an aspect of coolness to the otherwise sweltering landscape. The trees were so densely packed together that some of their roots reached far out over the winding bank and into the dark water, coursing rapidly over volcanic stones as though still being pursued by the forces of erupting lava that once formed this river bed.

In his descent Henri disturbed a cloud of small blue butterflies. I caught one and asked Claude, who was watching me from the bridge, "What is the name for this in French?"

"*Papillon.*"

"*Papillon,*" I repeated, skipping down to the riverbank through more clouds of these beautiful creatures. "It's a delightful word." By the time I reached Henri's side, he had already finished washing his face and I only had time to splash a bit of water on mine before I had to race back up the hill to the jeep where he was already gunning the motor.

Leaving the hills and valleys surrounding Leopoldville behind, we crossed the Kenge plateau, which was made up of miles and miles of slightly rolling brown savannah, as far as the eye could see.

"Looks like ripe wheat!" I shouted to Claude above the roar of the motor.

"It's elephant grass. This plateau is antelope and buffalo country."

"That's what people hunt mostly around here, isn't it?"

"Buffalo, especially. If you have the money for the license. And the right gun. License alone costs $500. Good reason, too. It's not a sport for dilettantes."

"I imagine not. Not at that price."

"No. The government controls the hunt carefully." A few minutes later he added, "I had a friend who went hunting last weekend. He suddenly came upon a buffalo lying in the grass. It charged immediately. If he had not been an expert shot, he would have been finished. *Finished*, I say. Because after he killed it, he discovered it had been shot through the nose, probably the week before. And had been mad with pain for so long it charged to kill the first man it saw. You know," he turned to me, "a wounded buffalo can destroy a whole village in rage. Once one did, killing several natives, and the villagers then went after the hunter. And killed *him*. It was a Belgian, too. But the government did, *could not*, do anything about it."

Henri spoke for the first time. Staring straight ahead he growled, "Fools! Public menaces! *Those who wound and do not kill!*"

After that, not a word was exchanged between the three of us for a long time, until Henri startled me by suddenly saying in a voice barely loud enough to be heard above the roar of his jeep, "I had a boy who was using my gun to go hunting. I warned him it was too small for the buffalo but he wouldn't listen. Just a month ago he came out here and was cut into many pieces by a mad buffalo. In his village they all blame me. They say I told him to go. But it's not true. I didn't."

He said nothing more and I gathered from the set of his jaw

that he had no intention of adding anything further. I looked at Claude but could see only his profile. His eyes were turned away from us, staring at the passing savannah.

It was the dry season and this part of the Kenge Plateau had already been burned by the natives, exposing miles and miles of hard brown conical shaped hillocks, some as high as thirty feet. Claude turned to me. "Termites. Some of those mounds are thousands of years old. It looks like one vast cemetery, doesn't it?" He didn't wait for my answer and turned away adding grimly, "The difference being that underneath *those* tombstones, all is very much alive."

We entered the District Kwango and after about forty miles reached Bankana. "The capital of the Bayaka people," Henri informed me and I wrote it down in the tiny notebook I carried in my shorts' pocket, along with the names of the other places we had passed through. When we arrived at the next river he told me, "It's called the Lufeme." Here we stopped once again to wash our sand-covered hands and faces in its dark, cool water. The road had long since become like a desert track. The jeep often skidded and sank into the deep, powdery, rain-hungry earth but Henri didn't appear to notice and never slowed down.

While we washed, two natives brought the ferry from the opposite shore. It consisted of two wide wooden planks floating on the tops of six rusty pontoons, three under each side of the planks. This homemade ferry was propelled across the river by means of a pulley stretched high across the river and fastened to iron poles on each bank. A steel cable connected the ferry to the pulley and the two Congolese "captains" transported us and the jeep across as one would reel in a clothesline.

After crossing the Lufeme, we encountered hilly terrain once again. Twenty miles more and we stopped outside a village to eat some of the sandwiches I had brought. "Now what is the name of this village?" I asked.

"Kabuba," Henri replied.

"Why do you want to know all the names of these places?" Claude wondered.

"That's the way I am. I always want to know where I'm going."

"Don't worry we won't lose you."

"Leave her alone," Henri muttered. Claude frowned and went on eating his sandwich in silence.

"Have I said something wrong?" I asked.

"No. Not at all," Henri replied.

Later Henri came to a halt by the banks of yet another stream. "This one is called the Gambo," he said.

"Thank you," I replied and also noted it down.

Getting out of the jeep, I hit the top of my head hard against the iron bar that was part of the frame for a non-existent canvas roof. I felt in my hair for blood and, worried, Henri asked, "Is it open?"

"No."

"Good. Be careful. That thing is dangerous."

He asked for the thermos of coffee and then decided, "I think it's time we added a bit of rum to it, too."

The rum-flavored coffee felt good as I watched the soft red glow in the twilight mingle with the fires on the hills surrounding the distant villages. Silhouetted against this sunset, they appeared in danger of being consumed along with the burning elephant grass. "They burn the bush in the dry season for hunting," Claude explained. "The flames drive the animals into their nets."

Forty more kilometers from the Gambo, we left the savannah behind and began to climb. "Not much farther to the Kwango!" Henri shouted when we began to descend into a valley. Darkness fell. The road became rocky, narrow, and twisting, and the surrounding vegetation dense. It parted just enough to let us through. Looking up, I could see in the glow of our headlights monkeys swinging from tree to tree, from branch to branch above our heads.

Compared to the intense heat of the day, the night air was fresh, damp and cool. I began to shiver, hugging my arms. Claude reached back and pulled out a windbreaker from the supplies stashed in the back of the jeep. "You'd better wear this," he told me. I had brought a sweater, but not a jacket, never imagining the jungle could be so cool once the sun had set.

He helped me put it on and then asked, "Okay? *Ça va?*"

"Yes, thank you. *Ça va. Merci.*"

Once, after bouncing over a particularly large rock, Henri turned to me and also asked, "*Ça va?*"

"*Oui. Merci.*"

Nothing more was said before we reached the village of Tansuni. There were little fires burning in front of every hut and the entire population crowded around us as we jolted to a stop. Henri explained, "They are waiting for me three weeks."

He greeted the people with a few words in Kikongo, then made a sharp left among the huts. Everyone, yelling with excitement, ran after us, grabbing onto the jeep wherever they could. Soon Henri stopped in front of one hut, he and Claude jumped down and, with the help of many eager hands, started unloading things from the back of the jeep into the hut.

I hesitated. Claude explained, "It is his house."

Surprised, I shouted to Henri, "But you are '*en famille*' here!"

He smiled. "Yes, you can say that. This is my Kwango family. And we welcome you."

As I jumped down from the jeep, the crowd was all at once silent. Then a murmuring ripple of wonderment passed over them like a gentle wave on a lake as they realized Henri had brought a woman.

I put my bag down on the dirt floor of the hut next to all the other things that had been unloaded from the jeep and looked around. There was but one room, one wooden chair, a hammock covered with mosquito netting and two air mattresses.

Henri gave instructions in Kikongo to his two men, Oscar and Gabriel. Then he told Claude what to do in French and me, in English, to pack what we would need in the way of food into a canvas bag. After all was ready, he put on a paratrooper's jacket, a woolen cap and rubber sandals. I gave Claude back his windbreaker and he, too, put on rubber sandals. After pulling on a pair of jeans over my shorts, I put on the sweater I had brought and substituted my own rubber sandals for my sneakers. Looking me over Claude said, "I hope your sweater is enough. It can get very chilly out on the river, especially before the dawn."

Then he and I began to smear our faces, necks and hands with insect repellent. I offered some to Henri but he scorned it. "There will be none tonight. Too cold."

But Claude went right on smearing. So I did too. I also slipped another anti-malaria pill into my mouth, though I had been told they were to be taken only once a week and I had already taken one just before leaving Leopoldville. But I took another anyway. Just to be on the safe side, I told myself.

I followed the men outside the hut where the villagers were gathered around the jeep, waiting for me to appear in my hunting garb. Pausing in front of the headlights, I delighted my audience by putting on some lipstick, balancing my small compact mirror on my knee, foot resting on the mudguard of the jeep. "Okay, you crocodiles," I called out, "now I'm ready for you!"

With one voice, the villagers murmured their approval. Encouraged, I proceeded to take off my pith helmet and brush out my long hair. This amazed my audience even more. When I realized Henri and Claude were also watching, patiently waiting for me to conclude my silly performance and get on with the expedition, I quickly tied my hair back with my scarf, adjusted the strap of the pith helmet under my chin and joined them.

As the jeep got under way, heading toward the Kwango, the villagers once again descended upon it as though it were a subway train during rush hour. We didn't have far to go, though. The Kwango was at the back door of the village.

The first thing I saw was the pirogue: twenty-three feet long, two feet deep, and no more than two feet wide. It was black, carved out of the trunk of a great ebony tree from the surrounding Equatorial rain forest. Hewn by hand, the hatchet marks were clearly visible. A new eighteen horsepower motor gleamed white in the glow of the jeep's headlights.

The men of the village helped unload the supplies from the jeep into the pirogue. A can of petrol, a tool case, a set of batteries and my food and drink, while Henri and Claude fastened miner's lamps to their heads, as did Henri's head man, Oscar. Then they loaded their rifles. In addition, Henri and Claude strapped holstered .45 pistols around their waists.

Henri indicated that I should sit on the wooden bench that Gabriel had placed directly in the middle of the pirogue. Then he disappeared in the direction of the jeep and brought back a seat cushion that he put over the plank. "There. That will make it easier for you. It's going to be a long night."

The gently purring motor quickly brought us out to the middle of the river. Oscar sat on the prow holding a 100-watt searchlight in his hands. Henri settled down behind him on the tool case. Gabriel crouched behind me and behind him was Claude, at the motor.

Oscar and Gabriel were bareheaded and wore cotton shirts and threadbare shorts. Their only concession to the rigors of the hunt were canvas sneakers. Otherwise they, like the rest of the villagers, always went bare-foot everywhere.

Henri handed me the two rifles. "You're in charge of these. I'll tell you the one to give me. The small one is what we'll be using. The big one could stop an elephant. I've never used it before on a crocodile. It's almost impossible to shoot in a pirogue because it has such a kick it could knock you right over the side of a rocking boat. I always take it with me, though, just in case."

At that moment Oscar's searchlight, which had been scanning both sides of the river, focused on a mass of tree roots on the left bank. Henri grabbed the smaller rifle from me, shouting something to Claude, and we headed for the shore. I couldn't see what they had seen. Until, what I thought were the roots of a tree, *moved*. It was a crocodile. The eyes were indeed red. Small, burning red coals. Watching us. Oscar's light never left them as we circled several yards upstream and came back down with the current, moving closer to the crocodile. Oscar played his searchlight around the area. Henri hunched forward over Oscar's knee; his rifle aimed at the two red coals.

Oscar's searchlight went off and Henri's headlamp came on. It was a much dimmer light, focusing directly on the red eyes.

Henri, never moving, shouted something to Claude. We turned. But the turn was too sharp. The pirogue almost capsized. My already fast-beating heart threatened to leave me altogether, taking my stomach along with it. But we steadied quickly, heading in a straight line for the red eyes, closing in fast. A few yards from shore Henri yelled, "*Coupez!*"

The second Claude cut the motor, Henri shot. The night exploded all around me. The crocodile leapt into the air from the impact of the bullet and rolled off the bank and into the water at our feet. Henri threw the rifle back at me and drew his .45. He aimed it downward for a second but nothing moved. Then Oscar's headlamp came back on. He, Henri and Gabriel jumped into the water, now full of blood in the light of Oscar's headlamp. Henri grabbed the crocodile, holding it firmly by the neck, and Oscar hung onto the tail while Gabriel tied its jaws together with a cord. It was almost six feet long, fat and ugly. And it was dead. There was a neat hole right in the center of its skull, directly above the eyes. Once the jaws were securely fastened together, the men threw it into the bottom of the pirogue behind me.

My relief was overwhelming, making me almost as nauseous as my fear minutes before. Everyone helped scoop out the water we had taken in and then we headed back out towards the middle of the river again.

"Let me shake your hand," I said to Henri. "A perfect shot! What a perfect shot! *Fantastique. Magnifique.* Please give me your hand," I insisted.

It was cold, wet and limp but I shook it vigorously, saying, "I was really scared. Yes. I don't mind telling you I was really scared." I turned around and shouted out the same thing to Claude, though I couldn't see his face. Just the glow of his cigarette. "I was really scared!"

"Of course," said Henri. "The first time."

Within minutes Oscar's searchlight stopped bouncing over the water. Henri stood up. Never taking his eyes from the something the light had found, his hands motioned Claude to close in on an area not fifty yards from the one we had just left. "My God, not so soon," I said to myself. "I can't go through this again so soon."

Oscar's searchlight went out and Henri's headlamp came on. Claude targeted the pirogue toward the red coals. Without turning around, Henri reached behind for the smaller rifle I was holding and I put it into his outstretched hand. As we drew nearer the shore, I had to duck as we crashed through some low-hanging branches. We came so close to the crocodile that its red eyes became white. Not until we were almost on top of it did Henri scream, "*Coupez!*" And fired.

He reached into the water and pulled the dead crocodile out by its tail. "Small," he said with disgust as he handed it over my head to Gabriel. It was about two-and-a-half feet long. For a moment I believed I might last the night.

Then Oscar whispered something to Henri and all lights were extinguished. Claude cut the motor and the four men scrambled out of the pirogue. They stood motionless, knee-deep in the water, staring hard at the river ahead. Henri reached over and grabbed the elephant gun from me saying, "If the hippopotamus comes up in front of you, don't make a sound."

We waited in absolute silence. Motionless. The shrill screech of a nearby baboon pierced the night, hunting or being hunted, followed by the sound of a large creature crashing through the surrounding jungle underbrush. Then I felt something as big as a mountain moving under the water about five yards away. But it kept going, passed us and continued downstream.

When I no longer felt this movement, the men's lights came back on, carefully searching the surrounding waters. Satisfied that all was well, Henri lowered his big gun and signaled for the others to return to the pirogue.

As we headed out for the middle of the river he asked me, "Had you fear?"

"Yes . . . . But, Henri, why were *you* frightened? It's shallow here. We wouldn't have drowned. And they aren't man-eaters."

"No," was his grim reply. "But we could lose the pirogue and all the supplies. It might be days before we would be found."

# 5.

## EL DIABLO

HENRI STOOD UP, hunching forward over the bow. Oscar's headlamp was focused on a circle of marshy grass and dripping tree branches, some dead and some alive, extending several yards from the shoreline out into the river. Two eyes of fire looked up at us from the center of this ominously twisted tangle of jungle vegetation. Henri's hand reached back, motioning for a rifle.

"Small one?"

He nodded.

Relieved, I put it into his outstretched hand. Oscar's searchlight played around the area, around the red-hot coals. The crocodile was alone. Then he switched his light off in favor of Henri's headlamp and we closed in until the red eyes turned white. Henri shot. Oscar's headlamp came on. A tremendous green-yellowish body leapt like a dolphin high into the air. It landed back down in the water with a great splash and, roiling with fury, headed straight for us at an incredible speed. The waves it created rolled and bounced the pirogue up and down, side to side. Another shot.

"The big one, Elise!" screamed Henri, throwing his rifle, hot and smoking, back into my arms. Its shoulder strap got entangled with the elephant gun. I fell forward trying, desperate, to lift it free. The pirogue rolled dangerously. I was sure we would capsize, landing right in the jaws of the maddened monster attacking from the left side of the pirogue.

But Henri's hands were quick and deft. He grabbed for the big gun and lifted it high enough in the air to untangle it from the smaller one, aimed down at the giant crocodile and pulled the trigger. The resulting explosion was that of a cannon at close range and the pirogue shook perilously from side to side, taking in much water. The bullet turned the animal onto its back but possessing demonic power, the crocodile righted itself and was alongside me. At my elbow.

Henri whirled around, throwing the heavy elephant gun into my lap and, at the same time, withdrew his .45 from the holster around his waist. The crocodile was reaching up for me, jaws wide open, inches from my face.

He passed me the .45 shouting, "*Shoot*, Elise! *Shoot! Shoot!*"

Pistol in hand, I stood up while Henri crouched down and held onto my ankles to keep me from falling overboard on top of the crocodile. I aimed the .45 directly downward, between the eyes of the monster, and fired into its skull again and again and again until the pistol was empty.

The crocodile ceased thrashing. Its jaws closed. It flopped over onto its back. Henri rose up, releasing his grip on my ankles. He took the .45 from me, quickly inserted another clip, and put his arm around my trembling shoulders without taking his eyes or the .45 off the crocodile, waiting for any sign of life. In the light of his headlamp I could see the black river running red with the monster's blood.

We stared at the beast for a long time without saying a word, its yellow belly glistening in the lamplight as it swayed, lifeless, back and forth against the pirogue, floating in its own blood. I felt nothing. Neither wonder, victory, nor disbelief. I was numb. I was in a state of shock.

It was Gabriel who spoke first. He knew this crocodile. "*El Diablo!*" he exclaimed, struck with awe.

Once the silence was broken and the spell that the killing of this monster crocodile had cast over all of us was lifted, the tumult and shouting of orders began. Gabriel and Oscar struggled, using long, wooden-handled steel-pronged hooks, to turn Diablo backside up. Then they held his heavy head out of the water while Henri twisted his big knife through the hole I had shot through the monster's brains. And he kept thrusting it in until it came out under the lower jaw. Diablo was definitely dead. I reached out and touched him to make sure but pulled my hand quickly back. The body was warm and felt still very much alive.

"We'll tow it," Henri decided, "to a sandbank." For the crocodile was longer than the pirogue. "Come back and pick it up in the morning."

As the men were securing it to the pirogue, Claude exclaimed, "*Quite a show, eh?*" His eyes were shining and his body fairly jerking up and down with excitement, like a puppet on a string.

Finally, I was able to speak. "*Yes!*" I replied.

The men climbed back into the pirogue. Once underway, Henri settled down to face me, his back against the bow. I managed to light a cigarette with still shaking hands and offered him one, too. "Quite a fight, yes?" he asked, drawing deeply on his cigarette.

"*God!*"

"You did *well*, Elise. I couldn't have finished him off. The angle was wrong. The .45 bullets would have just bounced off the side of his skull. You did well."

"Thank you." I was deeply grateful for his fervent praise. Then I had to add, "But I messed up with the guns! The straps got all tangled up. If you had had the big one a moment sooner—"

"No. No. That's all right. You did *well*. It all happened so fast. You never know until you shoot what the size is going to be. *That* is the danger. All the eyes are the same size. I never expected this, though. One never even *sees* the big ones before the early morning. They are hunting now. You only see them around 4 a.m., lying on the bank, fat and lazy, their stomachs full of the night's kill. And they can see you, too, and go into the water so you can't shoot. You bring us luck, Elise. She brings us luck, eh Claude?" he shouted back towards the motor.

"*Bien sûr!*"

"Is it bigger than the one in the photograph in your living room?"

"I think so. But that one was a gavial. And this one? He is a man-eater. Man-eaters this size are rare and the skins more valuable. Yes. It's the largest one I've ever caught."

"How much will you get for it?"

"About 2,000 francs. $40."

"*Forty dollars!*" I shrieked. "You should tell them to come and get it themselves for that price!"

He laughed and called back to Claude, "She says that for $40 they should come and get it themselves."

I heard Claude laugh, too. Then Gabriel and Oscar followed suit. Soon we were all laughing together, louder and louder. The sounds of our hysteria echoed off the jungle walls and a pack of hyenas lurking nearby answered with spine-chilling howls. They in turn were yelled at by a troop of baboons. Somewhere a lion roared and soon the jungle night was alive with the sound of a hundred screeching monkeys. All witnesses to our great battle with El Diablo.

The men jumped out at the next sandbank, which was a long, narrow mound of mud into which they sank ankle-deep.

"Careful!" I called out. "It could be quicksand!"

They paid no attention and began with their hands, the grappling hooks and all their combined strength to push, drag, pull, roll and tug the beast up onto the top of the muddy mound of river muck. I soon got out of the pirogue to help as well.

"Five hundred kilos!" gasped Claude.

"Probably," Henri agreed.

"Five meters!" yelled Claude.

"Probably."

"Oh, no!" I shouted. "More. More. I'm sure of it. Six meters at least. I'm sure."

"No," both men replied.

"Five," Henri said. "The most."

When we had finally gotten Diablo to the top of the mound I asked Henri, "Won't the other crocodiles eat it if we leave it?" I was beginning to feel proud of our trophy and didn't want anything to happen to it.

"No. I don't think so. He's too big. And they won't dare come close enough to find out if he's really dead."

Gabriel and Oscar gestured excitedly over the behemoth before struggling back through the stinking ooze to the pirogue. But Henri lingered behind. We waited while he stared down at El Diablo. Then, using the handle of his grappling hook, he measured the length of the carcass before returning to the pirogue.

We were almost out in the middle of the river once more before Henri stood up, turned around and proudly announced, "Five and a half meters, Elise. Five and a half, Claude. Maybe even five and three-quarters, from the tip of the nose to tip of the tail."

"That's almost nineteen feet!" I gasped.

"Yes. And the record is twenty. Six meters. But that one was a salt water crocodile caught off the coast of northern Australia."

I felt behind me for the thermos of coffee and bottle of rum and managed to fill two thermos cups while never once letting go of the two rifles. First, I passed the cups forward to Henri and Oscar. Refilled them and handed them aft to Gabriel and Claude. Then I passed out chocolate bars for everyone and once again, cigarettes. I looked up at the sky. The stars seemed to be brighter, the wind cool and fresh.

"Do you know what the boys tell me?" Henri asked. "That crocodile is very famous all up and down the Kwango. Oh, he has eaten many. Many. They tell me that he ate the wife and son of the chief of their village on the day Queen Astrid died."

"Queen Astrid? The Queen of Belgium?"

"Yes. She was killed in a car accident."

"But that was years ago!"

"That's right. Queen Astrid died in '32. I would give Diablo probably one hundred and fifty years. Even one hundred seventy-five."

"Really! How can you tell?"

"It's a guess only. You cannot tell a crocodile's age. He has the same number of ribs on his back all his life. They simply get bigger as he gets bigger and stretch farther as he gets fatter. Not like a tree that adds rings every year. After it hatches, it grows about thirty centimeters a year for the first few years until it reaches two meters. Then it slows down. Did you know that the crocodile dies only when it is killed? I've heard the same is true of the whale. That it dies only when it's killed or is beached, or chooses to die."

Oscar leaned back from his perch on the bow and pointed to something ahead. Then it moved to our left—a good distance away.

Henri stood up. He shouted to Claude, "À *droite! Hippos.*"

"See them?" he asked me.

I looked hard in the direction of his pointing finger and said, "Yes." Though I was not sure whether I really did or if what I was seeing were just white bubbles of foam, placed far enough apart to be eyes, that the swift current scattered here and there over the river's surface.

Once satisfied that we had cleared the hippos, Henri settled back down on his toolbox and continued, "Diablo was very clever, too. He would follow a pirogue returning with fish. Just as the fisherman got out, he would overturn the boat and eat all the fish. When he got older and bigger, he would overturn the pirogue in the middle of the river and take the fisherman as well. He was even known to wait in the grass on shore next to a pirogue until the fisherman arrived. Then he would take him there. Right on land. Oh, that one has eaten many. Many . . . . "

Later I wondered, "How could they have known here when Astrid died?"

"In the Congo news travels fast, via the 'coconut wireless.' You'd be surprised."

"Strange . . . don't you think? That the queen dies in a car on the same day that another young woman, one of her subjects far away on another continent, dies in the jaws of a crocodile? How little we know, don't you think, with whom our fate is eventually joined?"

After a long moment he finally replied, "Yes. You're right. How little we know," he said in a soft and dreamy voice, as though he was remembering something that had happened long ago. And then he turned his gaze away from mine to stare silently out at the river rippling by.

A little later I asked, "Why do they call him El Diablo? That's not French. That's Spanish for devil. *Diable* is French. And Diablo is not a Kikongo word either, is it?"

"No. But we are close to the border with Angola. Portuguese, you know, and Spanish and Portuguese are similar. Maybe it was the Portuguese who named him. He roamed far on this river and the Kwango flows into Angola. Oh, Diablo has taken many."

I remembered Yves Quero telling me of a group of Belgians fishing one Sunday in the Congo near Leopoldville. They were just standing in the shallow water by the shore holding their rods out before them while their wives and children played on the bank behind. Suddenly one of the men screamed, "I've been taken!" as he disappeared under the water.

This phrase kept resounding in my brain as we continued on. *"I've been taken. I've been taken."*

I struck a match, looked at my watch and saw that it was just forty-five minutes since we had left Oscar and Gabriel's village. It seemed like forever. Henri turned sharply around. "Give me the guns!"

I froze.

"Don't worry. There's nothing. But with all the excitement, I've forgotten to reload them. That must never happen again."

"For God's sake, Henri. Tell me about them in case I have to use one, too. I've wanted to ask you before, but it's always been too late."

He didn't understand.

"The rifles! I mean what does one do to shoot them? Where are the safety catches?"

"Oh, yes. Well, this smaller one is a .16 gauge, only I use bigger *balettes*. It's not for the large crocodiles. But I use it whenever I can. It's cheaper. I really should not have used it for the first crocodile but I had to because of the position. Here. Feel this."

I leaned forward to feel the movement of the safety catch.

"Now this one," he explained, taking the big rifle out of my embrace, "is a .440 magnum."

"The elephant gun."

"Yes."

"And don't you try to use it. It would knock someone your size right out of the pirogue."

"Don't worry! I won't."

"I bought it in Belgium," he recalled as he reloaded it. "When I heard I was coming here, I went to the best shop. You can buy the best arms in Belgium. In the States you know nothing of such guns. But they wanted 24,000 francs for it. $500. Then I found out that it was just one little man who made them for this shop. All by himself. So I went to him and asked him to make me one.

"He loved it. You know, he *loved* it. Loved knowing that he was making something to be put directly into the hands of a hunter. '*For yourself?*' he asked me. '*You are a hunter?*'

"And when I told him it was for the Congo, he couldn't do enough. He worked long on it. And only charged me $180. Just imagine that poor man," he said, handing the loaded .440 back to me, "working in that country where the sun barely shines and never knowing what happened to those guns he loved."

The pirogue stopped abruptly in the middle of the river. Oscar's light held another pair of red eyes in its hypnotizing glare. Henri carefully got out and sank in the water up to his knees. Fear took a firm grip on my guts once again as I watched him wade stealthily forward towards the red eyes, his head down, his back hunched over the barrel of the .16-gauge rifle. The others remained in the pirogue, silently watching. Oscar held his light firmly on the eyes, then flashed it in a semi-circle around them, then back into their fire.

"Henri! Don't! Come back!" I cried out, despite my resolve to remain silent like the others.

He stopped, looked back at the pirogue for a moment, then continued on wading through the water in the direction of the red eyes. He waved his hand, signaling to Oscar, who extinguished his powerful searchlight. Henri switched on his headlamp. Its dim blue light in the darkness of the night cut a direct path to the two red eyes, making their evil glow even brighter.

I felt the movement of the others slip noiselessly out of the pirogue. Claude lifted the elephant gun from my arms. The men followed stealthily behind Henri, spread out in a semi-circle. Claude with the .440 magnum. Oscar with the grappling hook in one hand and his machete in the other. Gabriel had the other hook and Claude's .45, while Henri slowly, stealthily waded through the shallow water, getting closer and closer to the red eyes, until I imagined they were laughing at him.

Then came the shot from Henri's .16 gauge, a splash, followed by many more splashes as the men now raced through the water towards him. Two more shots, this time from Henri's .45. Then the men bent over to pull the big crocodile out of the water as Henri watched. And waited. Pistol aimed downward until the crocodile's violent death throes ceased. Then Henri turned and headed back towards the pirogue. The others followed, carrying between them the dead six-foot-long trophy.

I yelled at him, "Why did you do that? There could have been others around!"

He smiled. "Rarely do they travel together at night."

After we were once more under way he added, "In the middle like this, we would have lost him if we had gone any closer with the pirogue."

We went on, sometimes swiftly, sometimes slowly. We circled. Closed in. Killed. Stopped. Went forward again, circled, closed in, killed, stopped. Again, and again, and again. Henri never missed. When he decided to head back down the river in the direction of the village, we didn't have to circle anymore. We were with the current and could close in directly for the kill.

Henri never shot until we were almost on top of the red eyes. And he was so quick that only three crocodiles were quicker than he, slipping their heads under the water before they had Henri's bullet in their brains. He never shot when this happened. He just lowered his gun and signaled for us to go on. Three other times he waved us away when he could see that his prey was very small, explaining, "It's only a baby."

Meanwhile, I would often hear jumping and twisting behind me in the pirogue: the latest kill in its death throes. Gabriel, sitting behind me, was crouched over the pile of them stashed in the bottom of the pirogue and ended the animal's misery with his knife through its brains.

There was one small one that wouldn't die, though. He moaned strangely as he twisted out from under Gabriel's knife and lunged for the canvas food bag under my seat. Within seconds he had clawed through it and was between my legs.

Gabriel quickly passed me his knife. I plunged it again and again through the hole Henri had shot between its eyes. The moans became louder, more desperate, and finally pitiful before it stopped moving.

I felt like a murderer. But the men laughed.

"Strange," said Henri, "I've never heard them cry before. I've heard them howl during the mating season. I've seen their tears, yes. But *heard* them actually cry like a baby? Never."

Again and again he killed. Afterward I passed out the rum, coffee, chocolate, cigarettes. When the rum was finished, I opened the bottle of cognac.

Around 1 a.m. I began to shiver. Not from the cold but from fatigue, although I had never felt so wide awake. Henri noticed and told me, reaching into his toolbox, "Here. Put on this." It was his sweater, which I put on over my own.

By 2:30 a.m. we had thirteen crocodiles. Henry asked, "Shall we try for fifteen? Fourteen is the most I have ever caught in one night."

"No!" I replied. I was determined that we would surpass all records. "Sixteen!" I suspected it was also the cognac that was talking. Turning around to Claude at the throttle, I called out, "Sixteen, Claude, okay?"

Henri chuckled. "She says sixteen, Claude."

And he agreed. "Okay. Sixteen," he said, sounding very sleepy, while I felt as though I had, up until this hunt, been sleeping all my life and had only just woken up.

Henri killed his sixteenth crocodile in the middle of the river, walking in after it like he had done with the fourth. This time I kept still and only yelled out when I thought I saw a pair of hippo eyes to his left, closing in on him as he went after the red ones ahead. But they were only specks of foam.

# 6.

## THE MAN WHO COULD SPEAK
## TO THE HIPPOPOTAMUSES

T HE PIROGUE MOTOR began making strange sputtering noises, as though it was choking to death. There was a sandbank not far away and Henri signaled to Claude. "Let's pull up there and check on her."

It was a good-sized bank, about thirty feet long and twenty wide, and hard enough for us to walk on without sinking into the ooze below its surface. Once Henri was satisfied that the motor was again in working condition, with sparkplugs changed, I suggested, "It's time for a picnic. What say you?"

"Good," Claude agreed. "I could use the break."

Delighted, Oscar and Gabriel grinned like two little boys at a birthday party as I opened my canvas bag and started pulling out the sandwiches. All of a sudden Gabriel disappeared but returned shortly with a wooden bench. It was my seat that he had lifted out of the pirogue and which he plunked down in the middle of the sandbank at its highest point so I wouldn't have to sit on the wet ground. And there I sat, enthroned, with the men at my feet, eating sandwiches and drinking cognac and coffee at 3 a.m. on a sandbank in the middle of the Kwango River in the heart of Africa.

"How far away," I told Henri, "the 'shore world' seems now. A sailor once told me that when he was at sea the importance of everything else—the 'shore world' he called it—faded into absurdity. It's true, don't you think? Even though this isn't the sea, only the river?"

Henri nodded, got up and walked slowly away from the group, smoking. Gabriel and Oscar soon followed him, leaving me alone with Claude.

Glancing over at the crocodiles piled up in the pirogue he said, "Amazing how much power is in their jaws. Up to 1,500 kilos of pressure. Even baby ones. Once, hunting on the Ubangi, when he first arrived in the Congo, Henri caught a baby crocodile about twelve centimeters long. He brought it home alive and put it in the living room in a wooden crate. In those early days Henri would inject the baby ones with formaldehyde and give them away to his friends as souvenirs. Formaldehyde does a better job than what any taxidermist can do. It dries up the insides without changing the crocodile's shape. According to his wife, you can even hear it cracking as it dries."

"*Ugh.*"

"Yes, well, that night she heard some noise and when she reached the living room, she saw that the crocodile had eaten through the crate and was in the process of demolishing the rug. She held a pencil in front of it, trying to coax it into the bathroom. It just snapped the pencil in two. Then she tried holding a big brass lamp in front of it. In one bite the crocodile crumpled it up like paper. And it was just a baby, remember? Well, at that point she called Henri, who got hold of its tail, and they put it into the bathtub. His wife, though, she felt so sorry for it she had the houseboy take it back to the river the next day and throw it in. 'It was only a baby,' she said. But Henri was furious," he concluded, just as Henri strode rapidly toward us.

He spoke to me carefully, this time in French. "Now listen, Elise. Don't be frightened. But we are surrounded by hippos. Completely surrounded."

Claude jumped to his feet. I remained seated, looking up at Henri, not sure I understood him.

"Maybe we have talked too much," he said. "But there's nothing to be done now. There are too many of them. Three hundred, maybe. We can only wait until they decide to go away. But try to speak as little as possible. Remember, there is nothing to be frightened of. They are curious. That is all. But they could become belligerent if we hurt one. Such a large herd does not frighten easily."

Claude switched on his headlamp and turned slowly around in a complete circle. Hundreds of pairs of bulging white eyes were watching us. Those closest to the edge of the bank were out of the water and I could see the hippos' heads. Their small ears were twitching back and forth. They were listening to us. The pairs of eyes extended on and on far out into the blackness of the moonless night. Clouds had covered the stars. The only light came from those hundreds of pairs of white eyes shining in the beam of Claude's lamp. Those farthest out, on the edge of the circle where the river was deep, floated on the surface of the water. It was the same on all sides of me: in front, behind, to my left, to my right. They were perfectly still, yet the bulk of their presence now created waves that rolled over our feet. They did not remain silent, however. As we stood and faced them, they began to talk to each other, making grunting noises.

Henri whispered, his voice intense and grim, "I don't know how it happened. This has never happened before. Damn! What a waste of time. God knows how long we'll have to wait."

The five of us crouched together in a circle. Watching and waiting. I poured more cognac into a cup and passed it around. Henri's elephant gun was by his side, ready. Oscar had the rifle. Gabriel held his machete. Claude gripped his pistol. I had Henri's .45.

"There really are *too many*," Claude whispered. "Up on the Ubangi there are so many they block the river and the boats can't get through. Yet, it was the government itself that pushed through the law protecting them."

"Why?"

"Well," Henri answered, "if it weren't for the hippopotamuses there, and in many of the other smaller rivers in the Congo, the steamboats couldn't get through in the dry season. Too many sandbanks and bars. They trample up the beds of the rivers so much they create a path for the boats."

Claude leaned closer to my ear hissing, "But they've gone too far! They've been protected too long!" He was frightened.

"*Quiet*," ordered Henri.

And we waited.

After fifteen minutes Oscar suddenly laid down his gun, got slowly to his feet and walked a little distance away from us. He stopped directly in the center of the sandbank, at its highest point. Henri, watching, started after him but halted as Oscar began to chant. A high-pitched wailing at first. Then his voice became soft and sweet, like the voice of a mother singing a lullaby to her baby. Gabriel, who followed Henri, stood next to him, petrified. His emotion was so great that he reached for Henri's hand and held onto it tightly.

Claude and I stood up, too. He whispered to me, "Yes. I have heard it said that Oscar is a man who can speak to hippopotamuses."

Then, without warning, Oscar's voice abruptly assumed a tone of great authority. It was as though he was on a stage in a darkened theater delivering a sonorous soliloquy. The white eyes of the hippopotamuses were trained on him like footlights.

Their grunting ceased. Their ears twitched wildly back and forth while Oscar continued to speak, half-chanting, in the firm, proud manner of a leader of men.

"What is he saying?" I whispered to Claude. "Can you understand?"

"Some. He began by telling them all about himself. Who he is, where he comes from, who are his ancestors, his chief, his father and mother, who are his brothers and sisters. And he told them Gabriel's history as well. Now he is talking about Henri. He says, 'Here is Monsieur Henri. A great man. A great hunter. He has killed hundreds of crocodiles for you. And you know how he killed the old bull you banished from your tribe that was attacking your wives, your young bulls. He fears nothing. He doesn't want to hurt you. So be . . . reasonable . . . and go away. Because if you don't he will kill you. *All of you.* He comes with a cannon from the big city. He has secrets. He *knows* you. So be good. Go away. Terrible things will happen if you don't go."

Claude paused. Oscar's tone of voice had changed. It had become softer, more conciliatory. "What is he saying now?"

"He's talking about you. He says, 'This time your friend the hunter has brought you a young woman from a great distance, from a country which lies across a wide ocean you have never seen. She is a good woman and has bought a wife for one of us—'

"What does he mean?" Claude whispered in my ear. "'*You have bought a wife?*' Have you?"

"Well, yes . . . . "

"When did you do that?"

"My God, how does he know?"

"They know everything about us. Well, did you?"

"Yes. I guess so."

"Why? Why would you go and do a thing like that?"

"Well! After I arrived, André—he is one of my assistants— came to me and asked me to lend him $150 so he could pay the marriage price for his wife. They just had a little baby boy and, without paying her father, they couldn't live together. Not with any honor. Or go back to their village. Because he works in Leopoldville, André had no cattle to pay with. And he couldn't do it on his salary. Not all at once, anyway. But he keeps paying me back. Faithfully. Ten dollars a week."

"You really are a strange woman . . . . And I'm beginning to believe a dangerous one, too." He squeezed my hand, murmuring, "But with a soft heart. I can see how this assistant of yours recognized that the moment you arrived and took advantage of you right away."

"That's what the consulate told me. But what do I care? What do they know? Besides, what else could I do? Work with a man all day that's miserable because he can't pay for his wife? I wish that the price of honor was that cheap where I come from—"

"*Quiet*. He's now telling them that you have killed El Diablo for them. 'She is tired,' he says. 'She must return to her own country, to her own village that lies far away on the other side of this great ocean, which you have never seen.'"

Claude stopped translating. Oscar continued his harangue, while Claude strained to listen, staring up at Oscar who stood tall, looking down on the hippos, gesturing emphatically as he lectured them. "Now he's talking about me," Claude murmured, with a touch of wonderment in his voice. "He talks about the bank. How powerful I am in charge of all that money. He says, 'But now this white hunter with all the money must return to his own country, too. For there is a woman there awaiting his—'"

Claude turned and faced me, eyes wide with chagrin. "*He knows.*"

"*What?*"

"She's told him!"

"Who?"

"Henri's wife."

"I don't understand."

"It's *she* who is awaiting my baby."

His voice was so choked with emotion it was as though he was being strangled. He staggered away from my side to sink down onto his haunches into the primeval mud.

"God . . ." I groaned and glanced quickly over at Henri, wondering what was the greater danger. These hippos or these two men. Gabriel was still clutching Henri's hand, and they stood unmoving, at attention, staring hard at Oscar. I felt fear as never before. And I hated Claude for not having told me the whole truth about his relationship with Henri. At the same time I knew I had to remain calm. Pretend I knew nothing. They could not destroy each other, and me along with them, as long as I remained between them. As long as I remained calm.

Oscar went on and on, sometimes shouting, sometimes singing, sometimes chanting, sometimes wailing—gesturing about wildly, chanting in a voice loud and deep enough to explode the lungs of any ordinary man. Then abruptly stopping to speak softly. *Very* softly. As he did this, I noticed some movement in the water. Almost imperceptibly at first, but, yes, the hippos were moving. Turning around and leaving. Yes. It was definite. They were leaving. First, four of them moved off. Four from the outer edges of the circle they had formed around the sandbank. Then, slowly, ever so slowly, four more followed. Then more. And more. Yet Oscar kept on talking to them even when they were all gone from around the pirogue.

We waited until the surrounding water was clear of them all and the river still, without movement, once again. Only then did Henri raise his hand, signaling for Oscar to stop. The men hurried to the pirogue but Claude didn't move. I pulled at his arm.

"Come! For heaven's sake! Maybe she didn't tell him. Maybe Oscar just *knows*. You said they know everything, didn't you?"

He stared at Henri, who motioned for us to hurry up. Gabriel grabbed my seat and I picked up the sack of what was left of the food. Claude still didn't move. Henri ran back to us and, swooping up the thermoses, said to Claude, barely glancing at him, "Come along, you *imbecile*. Hurry up."

Claude got to his feet and followed us to the pirogue like a man made of wood.

We all helped to push off. Once underway and everyone in place at their stations, my nerves raw, I burst out laughing hysterically. "Quite a show, that! Quite a show! Oscar, you were wonderful. Marvelous. Oh, yes, so marvelous," I repeated, as Claude gunned the motor with excessive force.

I poured out a thermos cup full of pure cognac and told Henri, "Pass this on to Oscar."

"Yes," he agreed. "He's exhausted, poor fellow."

We headed fast downstream. Suddenly Henri turned abruptly and waved madly at Claude, shouting, "What are you trying to do? Kill us?" He was shaking with fury.

We swerved sharply, almost capsizing. Then headed in the direction of the other side of the river, far away from whatever danger it was that Henri had spotted.

Claude said nothing. Did not explain, did not apologize. I looked back but couldn't see his face, only the glow of the cigarette he was smoking clamped tightly in his teeth, while Henri remained standing, staring intensely over my head at him.

"*Rocks,*" Henri explained. "*Rocks,*" he repeated, sitting down once again.

As he spoke I could hear the sound of fast falling, swirling water coming from the place where we had just been. Henri said nothing more for several minutes. Then, keeping his eyes on the river, looking back now and then over his shoulder at Claude, he said, "That's what happened to me a few months ago on the Congo. I had gone out alone and went into some rocks. Ripped out the whole bottom of the pirogue. Had to stay on the bank for three days. Three days without food. Or sleep. After that I got another malaria attack. When I tried to sleep, the mosquitoes were in my nose, ears, mouth. I tried putting another bottom on the pirogue by ripping open the petrol cans but it wouldn't work. Finally another pirogue, fishermen, found me. A week later came the malaria. I was delirious for many days. Bad. Bad. It was bad. Rocks can be the most dangerous thing of all—"

He sprang to his feet again. A pair of red eyes was watching, waiting for him in Oscar's searchlight.

This happened three more times until, in the shadowy grayness that precedes the dawn, Henri killed his nineteenth crocodile.

As daylight approached, the river sent up offerings to the dawn in the form of cold, wet, wispy fog swirling and twisting skyward. As we sailed swiftly through this dream-like mist, I had the impression that we were being pursued from behind and were running fast into a nightmare ahead full of uncertainties. I shivered. Henri said, "We're lucky we're only getting this now. Sometimes it starts much earlier and it's difficult to see them. Too, it makes it so cold. Last time my hands were so cold I could barely pull the trigger. Really . . . . Can you see the hippos now?" he asked, pointing off to the right through the thinning fog.

Indeed, I could distinguish many smoothly rounded black mounds of what looked like boulders arching out of the water. Then I saw a few heads come up with eyes attached to these boulders, watching us as we went by.

"There must be fifty of them there," Henri said, grim-faced.

"Yes." But at that point it seemed natural that they were there. That we were all there. One with the river, the grayness, the time of creation.

It was 5:30 a.m. when the fog began to lift itself up from the surface of the river and dissipate, like smoke rising from a chimney, into the clear, crisp morning sky above. As the grayness on the river thinned out, allowing daylight to take over, so did the jungle change color as well. Massive silhouettes of dense vegetation as high as ten-story buildings were transformed into black shadows. It was only when the first rays of the sun were barely visible on the horizon that the luxuriant green of the trees was revealed. All was perfectly still. The world made not a sound. All the forms of life that existed in the jungle at night had gone to sleep. And the birds had yet to wake up.

As outlines took on form and shape and color, I recognized my river. Slowly at first, as the fog lifted, then all at once when the sun broke through the mist. I saw the rocks upon which we had almost crashed. The big, ugly, stinking mud banks we had avoided and the sandbars hidden under a few inches of water that we had often ploughed into. I saw the high, sheer cliffs, at whose feet we had killed one of the bigger crocodiles. And the massive, twisted roots of virgin forest trees with their hanging vines that extended into the water, among which we had shot other crocodiles. As well as the dank, grassy marshes through which we had struggled in pursuit of even more, including El Diablo.

As I watched this dawn rushing up on us from behind, I saw Claude clearly for the first time since the sunset of the day before. The stubble of his beard was black against his chalk-white face. Very tired, his hand lay heavy on the throttle of the motor. I waved to him, calling out, "*Bonjour*, Claude."

He smiled weakly, "*Bonjour*, Elise."

Gabriel, crouching at his feet hunched over the pile of dead crocodiles, was shivering and miserable in his thin, torn, brown cotton shirt. His face was the mask of the eternal Bantu: ebony-black skin tightly molded to the big bones of his face, with staring eyes devoid of emotion. He, too, was very tired.

Turning around, facing front once again, I saw that Henri's tanned face was now gray. And black where his beard had begun to appear. But there was no trace of fatigue on his face. Every muscle was as alert as when we started. The only change was the satisfaction in his eyes, the triumph in the set of his mouth.

Sitting high on the prow in front of Henri, Oscar's profile was even more classically African than Gabriel's. He held his tall, wiry body erect against the cold air ripping through his blue shirt that hung in tatters from his bony shoulders. He wore two pairs of shorts because the seat was missing from the outside pair. His features were frozen, his face numb, his gaze unwavering. He still gripped his now useless searchlight, as I continued to clutch the two guns. I asked Henri to pass him a cigarette.

As we rushed along into the morning five crocodiles saw us and slipped under the surface of the river. With the first light of day, Henri had given up trying to shoot them.

We headed for the sandbank where we had left El Diablo the night before. He was clearly visible from a distance—an enormous crown cresting the entire width of the sandbank. I had seen this picture before. It was in the Museum of Natural History in New York: an artist's conception of prehistoric times. Gray light. Twirling and smoking fog slowly lifting, like a curtain going up on the dawn of creation. Green-black jungle bordering a sinuous, fast-flowing, plant-clogged river. Hippos, massive and still as statues off to the right, while in the center of the painting lay El Diablo on top of a slimy mound of primeval ooze. Several exotic, long-legged birds were fishing off the far end of Diablo's sandbank. If it weren't for the now-and-then cries of these birds, I would have thought it all a tableau. Only the sounds of the birds confirmed it was real.

Large footprints in the mud told us that a few hippos had come up to Diablo in the night to have a look. As I helped the men secure him to the stern of the pirogue, I got a good idea of the fabled power of crocodile tails when the tip of Diablo's—the part I had chosen to lift—slipped from my hands and fell against my ankles. It almost knocked me down.

Once back on the river, I dragged my feet and hands in the water, washing the mud from them and smiling to myself, remembering how I wouldn't have dared put a finger in the Kwango twelve hours before.

# 7.

## THE VILLAGE TANSUNI

"HAIL!" I SALUTED Henri, as we approached the beach at Tansuni. "The conquering hero comes. The dragon slayer."

He nodded, with a shy smile of satisfaction on his lips. His eyes were fixed on the shore, where the young men of the village were waiting to welcome him. As we pulled in, many hands reached out to help secure the pirogue amid murmurs of awe when the men caught sight of El Diablo.

"They already know we got him but seeing is believing," Henri said.

"The coconut wireless?"

"The drums."

"I didn't hear any."

"You wouldn't. It's a special one in the hands of what you would call the 'communications officer' of each village. They beat it under water and the sound waves travel along the river, picked up by a code specialist, who then transmits the message to the next village, and then the next and so on."

News of our arrival spread quickly and within minutes women and children, accompanied by the older men of Tansuni, came streaming out of their huts and gardens, running toward the beach, many carrying long, sharp knives. Claude said, "There will be a feast."

Henri immediately went to work giving orders and instructions in Kikongo to his innumerable assistants. Twenty of the men made a big production of lifting El Diablo out of the water and up onto the beach as everyone, including me, shouted encouragement. Their strain seemed so sincere I wondered how just the five of us had managed to maneuver the great beast in the first place.

Oscar was sent to get Claude's camera from Henri's hut and returned dressed in a clean shirt, slacks, and glasses, ready to have his picture taken. Claude took pictures of him and Gabriel, who did not bother to change his clothes, standing astride the vanquished Diablo, encircled by the smaller crocodiles. One of the villagers held Diablo's jaws open as wide as they would go, while another stuck an eighteen-inch long knife upright inside that kept the mouth open. A human head could have easily passed between the bright white teeth, as long and as sharp as daggers lining both sides of the upper and lower jaws. Looking inside, I noted that there was no tongue connected to the great gob of pink flesh where the throat began. "So, crocodiles have no tongues in the Belgian Congo?" I asked.

Henri laughed. "Guess not."

"Like the monkeys in Zamboanga who have no tails."

"What's that?"

"Never mind. It's an old U.S. Cavalry song I know," I replied, proceeding to sing, dancing about, *"Oh, the monkeys have no tails in Zamboanga . . . Oh, the monkeys have no tails. They are strung up by their nails. Oh, the monkeys have no tails in*

*Zamboanga. Oh, the crocodiles have no tongues in Belgian Congo. Oh, the croco—"*

My audience grinned. Henri frowned. I realized I was getting slaphappy from fatigue and stopped my loony antics.

Then it was my turn to be photographed by Claude. With one foot placed triumphantly on Diablo's back, a rifle clutched in either hand, Oscar and Gabriel by my side, and a circle of admiring natives close around me, I invited Henri to join the group photo as well. With the camera clicking away I announced, "Now that's for Irene. No. *That's* for Irene. Now *this* one will really impress her friends."

"Who's Irene?" Claude asked.

"My little sister. I just got a letter from her saying, 'Dear Elise, Have you gone on a safari yet? If not, please hurry up. I've told all my friends.'"

Everyone laughed. My lunacy was catching. Claude took more pictures, with different set-ups with Oscar smiling and Gabriel looking infinitely serious. "Stand here," he instructed. "Go over there. Now do this. Do that. Sit on Diablo's back. Shake his hand. Irene will like that one, too."

With the picture taking over, everyone gleefully pounced on the crocodiles with their large knives. Ten men set to work on El Diablo, five on each side of the body. They were skilled and worked swiftly. Their blades were precision instruments in their well-trained hands. Henri didn't have to give orders. He just stood back and watched, sometimes walking up and down, stepping around and among the carcasses and the kneeling, squatting workers.

With one quick thrust of the tip of their knives, the men first attacked the backs of the crocodiles and started cutting lengthwise where the horny part stopped and the smooth, patchwork-grained skin began. They chopped off the heads and claws and, turning the animals onto their backs, peeled off the underbelly in one piece, taking the skin of the arms, legs and tails along with it.

Then they scraped the skins completely clean and free of all particles of flesh that might still be clinging to what amounted to the outer garment of the crocodile. There was no blood shed in the entire operation.

El Diablo. L. to r. Gabriel, Author, Oscar (with glasses), the hunter Henri.

Author hamming it up for posterity.

Diablo's powerful jaws.

Night's catch. L. to r. Oscar (with gun), Author taking a break, the hunter Henri.

Shaking hands with the Devil. L. to r. Author,
Gabriel, the hunter Henri.

As I watched the men disrobing El Diablo, I wondered what I could take as a souvenir of this memorable hunt. What I could drag out of a musty trunk when I was old and gray to prove to wide-eyed grandchildren that I had been here. "Do you think I could have one of Diablo's teeth? One of the big ones?" I asked Henri.

"Certainly. The biggest ones will be for you. But you must wait for them. After emptying the skull they bury it in the ground for about two weeks. When they dig it up the ants have picked it clean. Then they bleach it white in the sun. I'm sure the chief will keep this head as a trophy for himself. And the teeth will be beautiful. You will see."

"They won't forget to save them for me?"

"No. Not for you. They will remember. I will tell them now."

By 9:30 Claude announced, "I've got to lie down."

"Elise should, too," Henri said. "But first let's all have some breakfast."

Five fierce looking old men, with faces streaked with ochre and wearing only loincloths, were hopping around in a circle under a giant mango tree in the village square. The were clapping their hands and stamping their feet to the rhythm of a drum being beaten by another old man. The hair on his head was shaved into queer patterns and he bore painful-looking ornamental tattoo scars on his cheeks. Several women, dressed in full-length colorful *pagnes* and wearing elaborate turbans of the same material on their heads, stood around watching.

"Those dancers were here last night when we arrived. Have they been going at it ever since?" I asked.

"Sure," Henri replied. "They started when we were on our way, asking their gods for our safe arrival. They continued while we were on the hunt, asking for our success. Now they are celebrating."

Three women, one behind the other, solemnly followed us into Henri's hut. Each carried six small white eggs in a shallow earthen bowl. With a half-squatting bow and lowered eyes, they presented the bowls to Henri, which he then, equally ceremoniously, presented to me. "They are for you. It's their way of saying 'Thank You' for killing El Diablo. One is from the chief, one from the owner of this house and one from the oldest man in the village."

The women curtsied once again and backed out of the hut.

I looked at the eggs and shook my head. "I should cook them with the bacon I brought. But I'm too tired. Let's just finish off the sandwiches for now."

"*D'accord.*"

So I laid the bowls of eggs down carefully on the dirt floor and distributed the rest of the sandwiches.

After eating mine, I took some paper napkins and asked Henri, "Would it be all right if I take a walk into the bush nearby? Will they follow me?"

"No," he smiled, understanding what I needed to do. "I don't think so."

Two women bending over a cooking pot giggled as I passed by. Several others joined them and the giggles became shrieks of delight after I thought I had disappeared from sight.

When I finished my business, I found Claude standing outside the hut, listening to the tom-tom music coming from the direction of the great mango tree in the village square. Surprised that he wasn't already asleep I asked, "Shall we go see what's going on?"

"Why not?"

The music was being produced not from the tom-tom alone but from tin cans as well. They were compressed in the middle and contained seeds. Each man had one and shook it with slow, insistent, monotone measures as he hopped around the man beating the tom-tom. Delighted to see us, the men gestured for us to join them.

"You start," I urged Claude. "And smile!"

He frowned but somehow forced his stiff and tired limbs

to humor my foolishness. Within minutes I, too, was with him inside the hot, sweating, male circle, attempting to dance their dance. There was a certain ring of familiarity about it that I couldn't at first identify. But it wasn't long before I realized that, though the rhythm was slower, it was basically the same I had encountered in Tahiti the year before. I took the tom-tom from the drummer and beat out a faster rhythm. The man grinned broadly, revealing a set of snow-white teeth filed to a point, like a shark's. He knew immediately what I wanted to hear. And the villagers' delight intensified as I let loose with the dance I had learned in the South Seas.

"Where does this come from?" Claude asked, perspiring heavily, as he attempted to imitate my movements.

"Tahiti!"

"*Tahiti*? What were you doing there?"

"Running away!"

I stopped only once to take off my sweater and rubber sandals to dance barefoot. Claude, exhausted, dropped out to join the circle of women that had formed to cheer me on. I threw him his pith helmet.

When I stopped, the drummer returned to his native beat and, with my eyes and hands, I asked one of the young girls swaying on the edge of the circle to teach me how to dance as her people did. For almost five whole minutes we danced, face to face, languid and trance-like, to the hypnotic voice of the tom-tom and the accompanying melodic rattle of the tin cans. Her bare feet stayed flat on the ground, while her body moved up and down, back and forth, side to side, with the elasticity and suppleness of a rag doll.

It was only when I saw Henri glaring at me, his hands on his hips, his paratrooper's cap pulled far down over his forehead, that I suspected I was out of order and making a spectacle of myself. But when I stopped dancing, he pulled the tom-tom out of the hands of the drummer, squatted down, placed it between his legs and, with powerful expert flourishes made it speak to all of us in a very loud voice.

He, too, in the heat of the morning, had taken off his jacket and shirt and was now naked to the waist. His broad, sun-tanned chest was streaked with sweat but he kept on beating the drum as though it had a devil inside that was taunting him. He was smiling but at the same time his eyes were telling me to cease and desist.

On our way back to Henri's hut, the village policeman, looking very official in a new, long-sleeved blue shirt, khaki slacks and government cap stopped him. Snapping to attention, saluting, he gave Henri the soiled, crumpled white paper napkins I had left in the bush.

Henri handed them over to me. "He says that Madame lost them."

There was great pride in the policeman's demeanor. He had been able to return lost property to its rightful owner. And profound satisfaction was clearly visible on the approving faces of the crowd accompanying him in the execution of his official mission. I accepted the dirty napkins with equal solemnity and bowed my thanks, wondering when and where I could safely bury them.

We passed a woman bent over a pot cooking on an open fire. Some of the crocodile meat was simmering inside. Henri spoke to her and then said to me, "I told her we were going to take a sleep and to have the meal ready by 1 p.m."

While I had been dancing, all the meat not required for the day's celebration had been cut up into huge chunks and put on large platforms made of logs raised about five feet above the ground. Fires were beginning to burn slowly under the platforms and its smoke rose up in fragrant clouds, enveloping the meat.

Glancing over at the fires Henri explained, "It takes three days. Then a truck comes and takes it to Leopoldville for sale in the African market. There's more than 1,000 kilos there. Diablo alone weighed 650 kilos."

I saw Diablo's head a few yards away, outside the chief's

hut. The big knife was still separating the jaws, and two chickens were picking at the flesh inside.

Inside his hut Henri told me, "I'll take the hammock. You'll be better off on the air mattress."

The minute I closed my eyes I had the sensation of spinning, of rolling back and forth, from side to side, like I was in an empty, speeding subway train late at night after having had too much to drink. I sat up and told Henri, "I don't know what's the matter with me. I feel sick."

"Of course. Remember, you have been thirteen hours in a pirogue."

"That's difficult to believe. It seems like only a couple."

I could now understand why Henri advised me to take the air mattress rather than the hammock. Then, in addition to the rolling motion I felt, there was a buzzing and ringing in my ears as though I was inside a giant wasp nest. Henri and Claude were asleep long before I dared close my eyes without fear of throwing up.

I awoke to the tom-tom an hour and a half later. And it was like being half-dead, struggling to climb out of my grave back into the world of the living. Henri, already awake, recognized how I felt and said, "Sometimes it is worse to sleep a little. Come. There's a stream where you can wash. Perhaps you will feel better after that."

While Claude slept on, he led me to a place where clear, cool mountain water raced over flat, smooth rocks on its way to join the Kwango. "You'll be safe here. I have to see about the salting of the skins. Meet me at the beach when you're finished."

As I splashed in underpants and bra, my sleep-drugged brain began to clear. For awhile I just lay on my back in a shallow pool looking up into the canopy of jungle above, enjoying the play of filtered sunlight upon the broad, polished dark green leaves of the trees. For five full minutes a sense of profound peace wrapped itself softly around my heart and I marveled at this.

After changing into my clean set of shorts and jersey, I walked out of the shade and over to where the white hot noonday sun was burning down on the beach. It had turned the black Kwango into a sheet of glittering sliver. The village men were generously spreading the burlap bags of rock salt we had brought with us over the undersides of the skins. Then they rolled both ends towards the middle, putting more salt between each layer as they rolled, until the skin ended up in a ball. They tied the balls in place with papyrus cords and stuffed them into the empty burlap sacks that had contained the salt. It took three men to lift the skin of El Diablo. "Probably weighs fifty kilos or more," estimated Henri.

Claude showed up and the two men worked quietly together, loading the skins into the jeep. After the last skin was in place, Henri decided it was time for lunch. "Now we'll see how you like crocodile stew, Elise. It should be ready by now."

Someone had placed a low, round table inside the hut and covered it with a black and beige material made of dried grass tightly woven into geometrical designs. They were ancient Congolese patterns, yet very modern ones to Western eyes. The place settings consisted of three battered tin plates, knives, and forks, and the three crudely carved chairs that had been placed around this table were so high that when we sat down, the table came to our knees.

I served the crocodile stew from the pot the cook set down by my feet. Chunks of white meat swam in a red, pungent-smelling sauce consisting of palm oil, pili-pili and the tomato paste and onions that I had brought.

"Is it Diablo?" I asked Henri.

"No. This is one of the smaller ones. The tail. The tail is the best part."

After a few mouthfuls I decided, "It tastes rather like a cross between lobster and veal. It has the delicate flavor of lobster but the consistency of meat. Strange. But yes. It's definitely meat."

And it was definitely good. So good that we ended by soaking up the sauce with the French bread I had brought.

We said very little as we ate, thinking our own thoughts as insects buzzed about us in the heavy heat. From outside came the reassuring sounds of village life that all was well: the tireless tom-tom, the rattle-snake rustle of the tin cans, the cries of playing children, the giggles of young girls and the voices of contented wives and mothers now that everyone had been well fed. Claude spoke not at all. Finally, Henri leaned back in his chair and said, "You did well, Elise."

"Yes," agreed Claude. "I am proud of you."

I bowed my head and murmured, "Thank you."

"If you like, you may come again," said Henri.

"I would."

A few minutes went by before I broke the ensuing silence. "It must be difficult for you to divide your time between the bank and this kind of life."

"Oh," Henri replied casually enough, "it's becoming impossible. But . . . . One must choose carefully. It would be a big decision, in fact, to leave. One can only do this three, four, five years maybe and then it's finished. *Finished.*"

He sat forward in his chair adding, "There is, though, a company in France. A friend of mine just gave me the address last week. It seems to have very good conditions. If I could get some kind of a guarantee. Some kind of a contract . . . . I would quit the bank and do this full time."

He glanced at Claude with a sardonic grin, eyebrows raised. But Claude looked away. Henri turned back to me. "I would get a larger boat and work all the rivers in the Congo." He was excited now and spoke as though he had spent many an hour, many a night, thinking through the details of his plan. "With a larger boat I could take supplies for at least three weeks at a time. Yes. Two or three years like that and I could really make a lot of money."

"I can't believe it's a question of money—"

"Oh, yes! Certainly! You can see what a good night can bring. Of course, we were lucky. If there's fog or rain, or if the wind isn't right and the smell of the motor reaches them before you do, it's not so good. But if I could do it every day, not just one day a week—"

"It *can't* just be the money, Henri."

"No . . . . " He leaned forward and removed his dark glasses. I could see his eyes clearly for the first time. Extraordinarily large, they were gray and flecked with green like the sea on a stormy day. He looked at me intensely. "I love it. It's something I have to do. And it's not so often that one finds he can do something he loves and make money at it, too. Is it?"

"No, it's not."

He turned to Claude. "Of course, one must not be married. Or have children."

The two men stared at each other, unflinching, for a moment without end before Henri turned away, rose from his chair, put his glasses back on and walked to the entrance of the hut. With his back to us, he extended his arms touching either side of the mud walls, staring out at the village and its people enjoying the meat he had brought them. Then he walked out to be among them and left us alone together.

"You know," Claude murmured, "I understand." And I had to strain to hear him above the tom-toms and the sounds of village life outside the hut. "You are right. It's not just for the money."

I got up and stood behind him, resting my arms on the back of his tall chair as he continued to sit, staring out the door after Henri. A mid-afternoon haze had settled over the village and shimmered under the merciless tropical sun like the vapors of a steaming cauldron trapped between earth and sky.

"What do you mean?"

"In a way I feel sorry for him. The man is consumed by demons."

I looked up and suddenly there was Henri standing in the doorway. He had returned from his brief tour of the village. "It's time to go," he announced and started to pick up the bags on the floor and put them into the jeep.

I carefully wrapped the eggs I had been given in my sweater and filled the earthen bowls with my remaining chocolate bars and cookies. Outside, the villagers gathered around the jeep to bid us farewell. Chief Makuba stood apart, leaning on his carved ivory walking stick. He was a distinguished-looking old man with white hair and a proprietary smile on his lips as he watched over our departure. A brown wool army blanket from World War II hung from one shoulder and covered his gnarled, emaciated body in the manner of a Roman toga. An ancient, battered white pith helmet completed his uniform. Three of his wives, the women who had brought the eggs to me, stood next to him. I returned their bowls to them, filled with the sweets. "Tell them," I said to Henri, "it's for the children."

The chief looked perplexed but bowed deeply.

"Will they like it?"

"They don't know candy. But," Henri added kindly, "they will appreciate it anyway."

Before we roared away the crowd of well-wishers pressed closer to the jeep. Gabriel reached across Henri and held out his hand to me. Then Oscar, on the other side of the car, leaned across Claude and gave me his.

Chief Makuba was the last to bid Henri goodbye, thanking him for killing Diablo, for freeing his people from the monster that had stalked his village for so many years, and then he thanked him for the meat he had given his people. To me, he bowed deeply, removing his pith helmet in a grandiose gesture of esteem.

The villagers' cheers were muffled by the noise of our motor and the people who half-heartedly attempted to run after us disappeared in the clouds of dust and sand in our wake. We could still hear the beat of the tom-tom, though, even after we were deep into the jungle.

# 8.

## FOR WHOM THE BELL TOLLS

"LOOK!" I SHOUTED to Henri. "Look!" I shouted to Claude as we came out of the jungle valley and reached the crest of the first hilltop. I pointed to the ancient emerald hills in the distance rolling to the horizon under the vast blue sky. "How beautiful Africa is!"

I threw my head back and began to sing, *"How beautiful for spacious skies . . . . "* And I sang all the way to the Lufeme ferry even though the men couldn't hear much above the deafening roar of the jeep's motor.

We were warmly greeted at the ferry by scores of admiring natives. The news of Diablo's slaying had already reached them via the "coconut wireless."

Toward dusk we saw antelope on the Kenge plateau leaping with infinite grace across the narrow sandy road ahead and disappearing into the elephant grass. We also saw several families of jackals jump from the road into the safety of the ditch to watch us pass by. Signs of exhaustion were clearly visible on Claude's face and Henri drove recklessly while I, the keeper of the cognac, passed the bottle from one man to the other many times. I told Henri, "Your jeep might be running on diesel but we are running on cognac."

Henri stopped only once—to eat what was left of the sandwiches and finish the bottle of cognac. Looking at the night sky, I asked Claude, "Can you tell me if the Southern Cross is there?"

It was. Bright and clear.

When we entered Leopoldville, it was as though I had come from the back of beyond. What two months ago had appeared to be a primitive colonial city, now looked like New York in comparison to where I had just come from.

Henri stopped outside Claude's apartment house and I gave him back his pith helmet. We shook hands.

"Thanks, Elise. Thanks for everything."

"Oh, no! Thank *you*. I've had a wonderful time. An unforgettable experience."

"I'm glad, then. I will see you soon," he vaguely promised as he turned away to disappear into the shadows of the palm trees scattered about his lawn.

Henri helped me carry my things up to my apartment door. Tired and dirty, we stood in the brightly-lit hallway where I gave him half of the trophy eggs. He shook his head but I insisted. "They are as much for you as they are for me."

We shook hands. "You can go with me another time, if you wish."

"Thank you. When you need me. When you want my company."

"*D'accord.*"

And he was gone.

"How was your weekend?" Bill asked, strolling nonchalantly enough into my office the following morning. But despite his off-hand manner, he appeared worried. Agitated, even.

"Oh, fine. Just fine," I answered.

He rifled through my in box and picked up the latest report on Radio Moscow that Yves Quero had deposited there earlier. Among other things Yves' job was to monitor Radio Moscow's broadcasts beamed to Africa, most of which consisted of anti-U.S. propaganda. Usually outrageously ridiculous things like predicting that the biggest problem the U.S. would have to face within ten years was the use of drugs among U.S. youth. These drugs had names unfamiliar to me, such as marijuana, heroin, cocaine. Within twenty years Radio Moscow foresaw babies in cities throughout the U.S. sucking up drugs in their mother's milk. The sons and daughters of capitalism, they said, would destroy themselves. Mother Russia would not need to interfere. Capitalism would fall of its own accord and communism would triumph. No one paid any attention to their ranting but broadcast reports were nevertheless routinely dispatched to Washington.

"You don't look fine. What did you do? Where were you? I tried to call, but no answer. Stopped by. Saw your car but you weren't in."

"Spent the weekend with some friends. Okay?"

"Sure. But you missed the reception at the Belgian Information Office. Remember?"

"I'm sorry. I completely forgot."

"Celeste was worried."

"I'm all right."

"You don't look it. As though you haven't slept all weekend. Have you heard the news?"

"No. What news?"

"*Independence*! My God, where have you been that you have not heard? Belgium is suddenly talking independence! It could happen as early as next June. And I'm glad I won't be around to see it. As you know, I'm up for a transfer soon and I hope it will come through before then."

"But, Bill! *Independence*! That's exciting!"

"Exciting?" He slid into the chair next to my desk and frowned. "If you want to call *chaos* exciting. Between you and me, that's exactly what it's going to be. If Belgium or Washington thinks there's going to be a smooth transition here from colonial rule to a full-blown democracy, they're kidding themselves. What I predict is that all hell is going to break loose once independence arrives."

"What makes you say that?"

"They are not prepared! You know yourself they have only six university graduates in the whole country! And they will only graduate next June. On the *eve* of independence. And what have they majored in? Political Science! They haven't one doctor, lawyer, engineer or army officer. How do they propose to govern this vast country? With a nation of clerks? An army of privates?" He shrugged his shoulders wearily and then looked carefully into my eyes, "You could be coming down with something. Perhaps you should see a doctor."

"I'm all right," I insisted. "Maybe I'm just tired, that's all."

"Sure." He smiled briefly. "Did you hear what happened Sunday on the river?"

"No?"

"Some guy was water-skiing on the Congo, just north of here in the Stanley Pool, when he was taken off by a crocodile. The creature just reached up, grabbed his leg, pulled him under and that was the end of him."

"Lord, how stupid can you be? Water skiing on the Congo!"

"That's what this country can do to you. Drive you crazy with boredom. And this was an executive from Unilever, too. Someone who should have known better. Not just some young kid. But people take all kinds of risks here they wouldn't otherwise take under normal circumstances."

"I know . . . . But there aren't supposed to be any crocodiles left in the river around here."

"Who told you that?"

"Oh, somebody. A friend. But somebody who knows all about crocodiles."

"Well," Bill looked at me, hard. Questioning. All he said though was, "If you do decide to see a doctor, we have one on the payroll. His name and number are in our phone book."

"Thank you. I know."

Bill was right. I looked awful. I hadn't slept the night before.
And when I did it was to have nightmares. Crocodiles crawling
all over my room. Up the walls, across the ceiling.

Then I was running like Snow White in a dark and evil forest
where the trees became witches; the branches, arms; the knots
in the tree trunks, grotesque masks. I was lost and couldn't find
my way out. But it wasn't a forest I was trapped in. It was a jungle,
full of treacherous swamps and swift-flowing black rivers filled
with burning red eyes and enormous open jaws reaching for me,
ready with teeth like daggers to snap shut upon me.

Then I was on the river with the hippos. "There's one!" I kept
trying to warn Henri. He would search the area I was pointing at,
as he had done throughout the hunt, and then tell me, kindly
enough, that the object of my fear was only the foam on the river
surface. Or a mass of vegetation growing out of the water near the
shore. Until we passed or sailed through them, I braced myself
every time for an attack from a hippo angry with me for disturbing
its grazing grounds. Invading its river.

Then Henri and Claude were there on a sandbank
surrounded by hippos. They wanted to kill each other and I was
in the middle between the two men. Henri was coming at Claude
with his big knife. He wanted to chop Claude up into pieces and
feed him to the crocodiles and I couldn't save him.

"Do you have your own doctor?" I asked Barbara, my
librarian, on Wednesday morning. She was English, from Kenya,
but had been in the Congo for fifteen years.

She raised her eyebrows quizzically and sat back on her
high stool behind her librarian's checkout counter. "Naturally.
Why?"

"I have a problem, you see, and I prefer not to have to go to
the consulate doctor."

She smiled. "Oh . . . ?"

"It's nothing like that," I replied, returning her smile. "It's
just something I wouldn't want the consulate doctor to know about.

No need to upset anyone. It could just be a problem I'm having adjusting to the tropics."

My nightmares were getting worse. This time I found I was hallucinating and walking in my sleep as well. I had woken trembling, bathed in sweat, and on my hands and knees next to my bed with a kitchen knife in my hands, stabbing at crocodiles I imagined were under the bed.

But I dared not see the consulate doctor. I would have to admit I had gone on the hunt and he might find me a nut case ready for repatriation back to Washington.

"You should see Dr. Thomas. He specializes in tropical diseases. Been here forever. Thirty years. Forty maybe. Before that he was a General in the Abyssinian campaign. Served in Burma, too."

Thomas' office was in his home on a side street off Boulevard Albert. He was in his mid-sixties, short, plump, balding and greeted me suspiciously, with a guarded expression in his small, piercing eyes, as though *he* had something to fear from *me*.

After explaining what was happening to me, I concluded, "But I wasn't *that* afraid during the hunt."

"What kind of drugs are you taking? Did you take?"

"Nothing. Only my anti-malaria pills."

"How many?"

"Three. I know I should only take one a week but I wanted to make sure—"

He burst out laughing. "All at once?"

"Well, almost. Within a twenty-four-hour period."

"That's your answer. Enough to last you a lifetime! You'll just have to wait until the chemicals work their way out of your system. And until they do I wouldn't advise taking anyone into your bed with you." He leaned forward, squeezed my hand, and with the other provocatively ran his fingers gently up my arm. "In the meantime, if you get lonely, if you need rest, just come and see me. I can make you sleep."

I leapt to my feet, paid his fee and left him, an evil smile on his face. I heard him laugh as I slammed the door, thoroughly pleased with himself. Once back in my car it was my turn to laugh—with relief. It was only the pills! I was not losing my mind. I could join Henri again, as he promised. As I had agreed.

"Can't stay long," Claude announced, when I answered the doorbell that evening. He was excited, his big black eyes flashing impatience. "I've come to say goodbye. They're moving me out right away. Tomorrow. Sooner, much sooner than I had hoped for. The bank's truck will deliver the things you promised to keep for me. Maybe tomorrow evening or Saturday morning. Just think!" He walked past me and out the door onto the balcony. I followed. *"Finally getting away from all this!"* he exclaimed, extending his arm over the land and the river below.

"I'm glad for you."

"Mind you, Goma is not a promotion. But I don't care. Anything is better than this place."

"Let me make us a drink to celebrate."

"All right. A short one. I still have to pack."

I mixed a rum punch that we sipped on my balcony, staring down at the Congo. The stars above were so close it was hard to distinguish them from the blinking lights of Brazzaville across the way.

He sighed, "Oh, I wanted to change the world . . . . But when you see this river . . . . " Then lifting his head, his eyes to the sky, he continued, "Those stars . . . . You know it's useless. Not all the beauty in the world can make up for one unhappy soul."

"I know."

"On the other hand," he continued, "people have always been miserable and will always go on being miserable . . . . I have found a little peace now, at least. If not happiness, peace. And that is something to be grateful for."

He turned to me. His voice sank almost to a whisper, as soft and as warm as the tropical evening breezes wafting off the river below and reaching up six stories to caress our faces, our naked arms and legs. "You have helped me more than you know. I hope you will find some happiness."

"Thank you."

"Though you haven't told me, I know you have a story, too—"

"*Everybody* has a story. What counts is how strongly you feel about it."

"I guess so." He took a deep breath, then emptied his glass. "The Spanish have a saying," he said, "that not until a soul has left a body, two hours after its death, can you understand that somebody. Have you ever heard that?"

"No."

"It's in *For Whom The Bell Tolls*. Now I can only remember her smile . . . . That smile as she asked for a cup of coffee . . . in those few moments when she became conscious. I knew then that she was happy. It was her fate, I guess. That smile was the smile of one who has achieved her destiny. That's what I remember now . . . . "

"A smile . . . . Yes. A smile."

"If you need anything here, contact the bank."

"Thank you."

I then dared to ask, "Is it settled . . . with Henri's wife?"

"Not with her, no. Not yet. All I know is that I cannot marry her. I don't love her and I've made enough mistakes in my life already. You know," he turned to me, seeking out my eyes in the darkness, "she knew what she was doing. She wanted a baby so much. She became pregnant before she and Henri could get married and they had to have an abortion. She never got over it and was crazy to have a baby ever since."

"Why didn't she have one with Henri later? After they were married?"

"I don't know. Maybe she didn't love him anymore after the abortion."

"I see—"

"Try to understand," he pleaded, "after my wife died, she was the only intelligent person around here that I could talk to. Who could understand me and what I was going through. But then she fell in love with me."

"She will have to find her way."

"Let's not talk about that now."

"No," I agreed. "It's difficult to talk about things too close to us. One always needs time. Distance. To see things clearly. I guess that's really why I'm here. To see things clearly. And why you're going away."

"I know."

So we talked of other things and soon he was gone. I watched from my balcony as his MG went up my rocky dirt road, backfiring and protesting, as usual. But this time he drove carefully. He turned the corner well. He would be all right. He would be safe—for a while, anyway.

Bill Hart's transfer came through sooner than expected. "Dakar," he announced with much pleasure. "French. And I know the people."

He and Celeste were packing up, while the consulate hummed with exaggerated activity preparing for independence. We were being promoted from a lowly consulate to a full-fledged United States embassy. Gone would be the days of dealing with the stifling bureaucracy of the Belgian colonial government. We would soon no longer have to live with the ever-present fear of stepping on colonial toes, being declared a *persona non grata*, and expelled from the country. Which could also mean death to one's career in the Foreign Service.

I became busier than ever with receptions every night. The British ball, the Portuguese national holiday, the arrival of members of the War College, the director of the Voice of America, the Under Secretary of State for African Affairs, and U.S. journalists, all of whom had to be entertained and given tours of Leopoldville and introductions to emerging Congolese political leaders. Because of the sudden interest in African art, Bill and I were besieged by art collectors from museums around the world, including the personal representative of Nelson Rockefeller. The well-known photographer Elliott Elisofen also stopped by. He was putting together an illustrated book of artifacts from many areas of the African continent and was especially interested in featuring the Belgian Congo.

"Congo's independence will open up a new epoch in the history of Africa, with the United States as its friend. Communism might try to muscle in and Russia get its foot in the door but they don't stand a chance," predicted Paul Springer, the political affairs officer.

An independent Congo would be a democracy and it would be to the United States that it would naturally turn for advice. "Making favorable trade agreements, of course," Owen Roberts, the economics officer at the consulate assured everyone.

But the life of a diplomat held no more interest for me. The gossip, the dreams, the plans and intrigues whirling about me in the form of endless communications with Washington labeled *Confidential, Secret, Top Secret* became a burden to the point where I felt like I was being strangled as surely as if a powerful hand had a grip on my throat. I found myself in an air-conditioned prison set down squarely in the middle of ancient Africa and as isolated as an earthling would be on Mars. I sensed that I was participating in a 20th Century drama before an audience of 10th Century people who were mocking us as we played on, oblivious to the real world outside our big glass windows.

# 9.

## INVASION OF THE CROCODILES

"I'M PLANNING ANOTHER hunt," Henri called the following Friday. "Would you like to come along?"

"Yes," I replied, automatically, without thinking, without asking when.

"We will be leaving tomorrow. It's short notice, I know, but there's a new Unilever fellow arrived. He's about to be sent to the Kasai next week to manage one of their palm oil plantations and wants to acquaint himself with the territory before settling in. I told him about you and he wants to meet you. Young fellow. Single. Name is Jean Lauwerens, half Swiss, half Belgian. He's done some hunting in Europe and knows how to handle a boat. I don't think he speaks English, though."

"That's all right. I guess I can muddle through with my French."

"I don't know how good his French is either. He speaks Flemish and German."

"Well, I guess you'll have to translate."

"You might learn German," he chuckled.

I laughed with him. "Never! I'm having a hard enough time getting by with my French."

"Good. We'll pick you up at noon tomorrow."

"Shall we go up the Kwango?"

"No. This time we'll go down toward the Angolan border. I've pretty much picked the upper Kwango clean. Have to give it a chance to repopulate itself. Too many hippos, anyway. I don't want to run into the same thing that happened last time. Jean knows how to handle a boat in shallow waters but he's never had to deal with hippos in Switzerland. No. This time we'll go to Tansuni, leave the jeep there, hunt Saturday night and head towards *les chutes Guillaume*. You call them Williams Falls. I'd like to show them to you. They are one of the marvels of the Congo and certainly one of the most beautiful in the world. Something tourists rarely get to see because there's no way of getting to them except by pirogue. There's something of a road from Popokabaka to the falls but one can't really see them well from the road. You have to hike in through dense forest."

"I've never even heard of them."

"It's one of the Congo's well kept secrets. Then we'll head back to Tansuni Sunday morning."

"What shall I bring?"

"More of what you did last time. Those ham sandwiches were good."

"Thank you."

"And the tomato sauce and lots of onions for the crocodile stew I'll make us on Sunday. We won't have time to eat at Tansuni. Just time enough to skin and salt the hides. We'll have to eat on the way back to Leo. I'll bring the pili-pili. And, oh, yes, don't forget your bathing suit. We'll want to take a swim while the stew is cooking."

"*A swim?*"

He chuckled. "At least cool ourselves off. Clean ourselves up."

"This time I'll bring my camera."

"Good. And I promise to find us some crocodile eggs for Sunday breakfast. Bring along the bacon. That should be interesting. I don't think the boys have ever tasted any."

Jean Lauwerens was my age, in his mid-twenties, blond, with lively blue eyes, exuding good humor. He was not tall but had the build of an athlete. A good-looking man, he was eager to learn about life in the Congo. How to survive there and, at the same time, enjoy himself while doing so. "Until his fiancée arrives, that is," Henri declared. When we stopped by the stream Gambo to wash our faces, as we had done on the last trip, Henri whispered to me, "I didn't know he was engaged."

"Would it have mattered? Wouldn't you have asked me to come any way?"

*"Bien sûr."*

Henri, who had previously spoken only Flemish with Jean, was wrong about his language skills. We were surprised to learn that he did speak some French, even some English, and he and I managed to communicate with a few words here and there, accompanied by meaningful gestures. There was not much conversation possible, though, during the jeep ride to Tansuni because of the roar of the motor and the amount of dust we kicked up in our wake. It hadn't rained in months and the reddish-brown ground was very dry. This time I brought my own hat. It was a broad-brim straw affair with a cotton kerchief cleverly sewn on the inside. By tying the ends of the kerchief around my chin, my head was protected from the sun and my hair, neck, and somewhat my face, from the dust of the road.

At one point I managed to say, "It continues to amaze me that in a country as small as Belgium there are two different languages and one can grow up not learning them both."

Henri nodded, hugging the wheel. "Not only that but you can grow up in a town where one side of the street speaks Flemish and the other French," he said. "One side goes to a Flemish school and the other to a school where only French is spoken. There are more Flemish that speak French, though, then there are people of French origin who speak Flemish. I am Flemish but had to learn French to work in the bank."

"How did this happen? These two languages?"

"You don't know? Look, I'll explain later."

At the Lufeme ferry Henri began, "Well, it's a long and complicated story, but I'll make it brief for you. France, Spain, England and the Netherlands had fought for centuries over what is now Belgian territory. To settle these disputes once and for all, the kingdom of Belgium was created in 1831 by the powers that be at the time: France, Holland, England and Prussia. They sliced off a piece of northeastern France that was inhabited by the French-speaking Walloons and a piece of the western Lowlands in Flemish country. They crowned Prince Leopold of Saxe-Coburg king of this territory and called it Belgium. The Flemish and French have been fighting ever since over whose language will prevail."

"French are very proud," Jean added, understanding what Henri had said. "They don't speak Flemish."

"They don't like English either," I told him.

He smiled at me. A charming crooked smile. For a fleeting moment I felt a pang of regret that he was already spoken for. "I like English, but not English English. American English. Your English."

"And can you imagine?" Henri asked. "They send Flemish priests here who are teaching the Congolese to speak Flemish, when the official government language is French. A lot of good that's going to do them come independence."

"So that's what it is," I realized. "Now I understand why when I speak to my students of English in French, many appear not to understand. I thought it was because of my fractured French."

"No. The Congolese you are teaching won't admit to not knowing French. They can't get a job in the government if they don't know it. Yet they teach them Flemish! *Muleheads*."

The people of Tansuni greeted us warmly when we arrived at nightfall and before descending to the Kwango, we were treated to a performance of a folkloric dance outside Henri's hut. Four young men had put on raffia skirts and dabbed their otherwise naked bodies with white spots, in imitation of a leopard's skin. Running with sweat, their bodies gleamed in the torchlight as they danced about. Plumes of white feathers were wound around their arms and heads and they held small, flat, intricately carved drums against their knees that they beat rhythmically, with big, wide grins on their faces. "It's a dance of *rejouisance*. Rejoicing that we have come back," Henri said. "That *you* have come back. You bring them luck."

The women were clapping and laughing too, urging the young men on, some shaking seed-filled gourds in accompaniment to their drums. I clapped and laughed with them and then took pictures of the dancers, which delighted them, while Henri unloaded what he wanted to leave in his hut. There I pulled a pair of dungarees over my shorts, put on a sweater, hung my camera around my neck, and stuffed a jacket and my hat into my box of food supplies. I did not take any anti-malarial pills this time. The crocodile nightmares had stopped but I wasn't taking any chances of having them reoccur. I would never take another pill again.

Oscar and Gabriel helped Henri and Jean unload our supplies from the back of the jeep and into the pirogue. When we climbed in, Henri pointed to a carved, cylindrical stool set in the middle of the pirogue where my wooden bench had been the last time. "That's for you," he said. "They now give you the place of honor."

"Ah! My throne." He handed me the guns and we were off, heading south down the Kwango in the direction of Angola, this time Jean at the motor.

The hunt began almost immediately. Henri never missed, using his .16 gauge in every instance. The crocodiles shot were of all sizes but none more than six feet long. Whenever I could, I took pictures of the men pulling the animals into the pirogue with their grappling hooks before they could sink to the bottom of the river. Once I managed to get a photo of Henri as he jumped into the shallow water near the shore to finish off a larger crocodile with his pistol.

Village of Tansuni welcoming back the crocodile hunters.

Jean followed Henri's instructions in Flemish and handled the motor well, Henri pointing out where the rocks were. He warned him about upcoming floating logs, half-submerged sandbanks and how to navigate around them, including the occasional hippo. But Jean never volunteered to jump into the water to help Henri and his men secure a downed crocodile. He was feeling the same fear as I had felt during my first trip and spoke little, uttering only gasps of astonishment from time to time, asking me, *"Had you not fear?"*

"No. And you?"

"But yes!"

And I magnanimously replied, "Of course. Your first time."

Indeed, my stomach-churning fear had disappeared. On the contrary, I was enjoying myself more than on the first hunt, passing out cigarettes, coffee, chocolate, and the rifle. Henri and I worked in sync as I began to share with him and his men the thrill of the hunter's rush stalking and vanquishing his prey. The hypnotizing red eyes of the crocodiles became my personal enemy as well as Henri's.

By midnight we had shot ten crocodiles and I felt the cold of the night air enough to warrant donning my jacket. Jean and Henri did the same and I wondered at the stamina of Oscar and Gabriel as the cold, wet wind lying low over the river ripped through their thin shirts, causing their teeth to chatter. But this time Henri had come prepared for this as well. He pulled two windbreakers out of his tool chest and handed them over to his men, while I broke open the bottle of rum.

By 3 a.m. we had bagged a total of twenty-one crocodiles. Another record broken for Henri. Around 4 a.m. the river ran swiftly between high cliffs and became more and more shallow. Jean often had to lift the motor out of the water to avoid having it get stuck in the mud or scrape an underlying rock shelf. Soon I heard a distinct roar in the distance. For a moment it sounded like the uninterrupted noise, so familiar to me, of heavy traffic speeding along the Los Angeles freeway, or the crashing of storm waves against a rocky shore.

"We are approaching the falls," announced Henri. "Get as close to the shore as you can," he warned Jean.

Jean abruptly pointed the pirogue toward a clump of reeds where the forest ran into the river. Oscar shouted. His lamp held fast a pair of red eyes not a foot away, directly in our path. One minute more and we would have run over them. Henri shot. The crocodile leapt into the air. It was huge. And then it went under. Henri leaped out of the pirogue, his .45 in hand and shot into the water. Without thinking, I followed with the elephant gun, and immediately sank knee deep into the stinking, decaying muck of the riverbed. Jean reached out from the pirogue and grabbed me around the waist to keep me from falling, gun and all, into the mud and reeds, as the crocodile reared its giant head. Henri shot again and again with his .45 until he was satisfied it was dead. At which point Oscar and Gabriel were ready with their grappling hooks to hold it up.

"A gavial," Henri said. "An ancient gavial. Probably three and a half meters." He looked at me holding the elephant gun over my head. "Don't ever do that again," he growled. "I'll tell you when I need it."

"*D'accord*. I'm sorry," I shuddered, stepping carefully through the muck, praying it wouldn't suck off my rubber beach shoes. I wanted to get a closer look at the gavial. "My God, another monster!"

"They don't get bigger than that. Once again, Elise, you bring us luck."

"Thank you."

Then, he decided, "We'll have to find a sandbank where we can empty out the pirogue and re-stack the rest of them in the rear to make room for this one in the front. We can't tow this beast all the way back to Tansuni."

But there was no nearby sandbank. The river was running too swiftly toward the falls. Henri settled instead for a clearing in the reeds along the shore. He climbed up the bank, followed by Oscar, searching the area carefully with their powerful lamps. Then they directed their light into the branches of the trees above. Satisfied

Henri going in after a big one.

that there was no danger of more crocodiles snoozing among the roots of the trees on shore, and no leopards ready to pounce on us from above, we pulled the pirogue up onto the land. Although he at first shrank from the touch of the crocodiles' wet, cold, slimy bodies, Jean helped us empty the pirogue. And it took the combined strength of all of us to drag the monster gavial up onto the shore.

"How can you tell it's a gavial?" I asked Henri. "What's the difference between a gavial and a crocodile?"

"Look at how pointed the jaw is, as compared to the jaws of the crocodiles. And how long it is. And look at the teeth. See how sharp they are and how they interlock. A very efficient fish-catching mechanism. If you count them there should be twenty or twenty-one on each side of the upper jaw. All about the same size."

He was right. And the teeth looked like they had been filed to a point. They were so sharp I almost cut my finger touching one.

"On the other hand," he said, turning over one of the larger crocodiles we had shot, "the crocodile has more of a square snout and the fourth tooth in the lower jaw fits into a notch *outside* the side of the upper jaw."

Yes, I thought, that's one of their features that gives them such a formidable appearance when you see them floating in the water, just the snout sticking out, the eyes looking at you . . . . Until they suddenly raise their snouts and you see those dinosaur teeth.

We reloaded the pirogue, stacking the smaller crocodiles behind me where Gabriel would sit on top of them, and heaved the gavial into the mid-section, tail under my feet and head in the bow. With this done, Henri decided, "Might as well stay here until morning. Dawn's almost up, anyway. No use hunting any more. Pirogue's full."

Jean breathed a sigh of relief. "*Bien.*" As did I. We were both very tired.

"With sunup we can have breakfast, get a look at the falls, and then head back to Tansuni."

Author examining crocodile's teeth.

Henri unrolled a woven reed mat on the ground and told me and Jean, "Lie down and get some rest. I'm going with Oscar to take a look around. Maybe find you some crocodile eggs, Elise, for breakfast, like I promised. Gabriel will keep watch."

Once my head hit the mat, I felt the ground trembling faintly under me as the power of Williams Falls in the distance sent shock waves of sound through the earth, as would an earthquake. Jean huddled next to me. When Henri woke us up an hour later, we hadn't moved. The sun was already burning through the wispy fog rising from the river, shining in my eyes like the glare of an oncoming headlight as seen through a dirty windshield. Henri was smiling as he looked down on us, holding out his cap containing five large eggs.

Gabriel had a fire started already. Henri handed him the eggs while I stumbled down to the river, splashed some water on my face and rinsed out my fuzzy mouth. As Gabriel was watching over the frying bacon, Henri brought the strange stool from the pirogue and set it down on the bank for me to sit on. "It's called a taboret," he said. "And is created only for women of standing. They carry it with them when attending formal ceremonies and sit a certain way as they have been taught. Like this." He sat down with his legs at a sharp angle, knees joined, chest held high, shoulders back and both hands placed on the knees. "Most important is the facial expression. It must be vague, eyes vacant, avoiding direct contact with the person one is having a conversation with or with any passerby."

He slowly passed his right hand over the entire surface of his face, from his forehead to his chin, closing his eyes in the process. When he opened them they were expressionless—dead and vacant. Nothing in his appearance could betray the truth of his real feelings. By passing his hand over his face he effectively wiped out any emotion that might have been there, as surely as does an eraser passing over a blackboard.

"Some white men assume that look, too," he added, "when they've been here a long time and have had to deal with the natives. You'll see. It works well in many instances. Especially when they're in a difficult spot or having to decide, confront or pass judgement on unpleasant issues. Eventually it becomes part of their nature. They don't even know when they're doing it. Come," he rose from the taboret, "I'll show you what a crocodile nest looks like."

There was a steep path leading up from the clearing into the forest. "Where's Oscar?" I asked.

"He went on ahead to explore. Perhaps find us some wild bananas."

The path looked well worn. "A crocodile walk?" I asked, joking.

"Yes."

"Oh!"

He laughed. "There could be a village nearby."

We soon came to a small clearing in the bush by the side of the path and Henri stooped before a large mound of vegetation in the middle of this clearing. "Just think," he murmured, half to himself, half to me, "crocodiles are the direct descendents of the dinosaurs. They date back to the Jurassic period millions of years ago. A cataclysm of some sort wiped the dinosaurs out but not the crocodile."

"Well!" I exclaimed, sitting back on my heels next to Henri, "that settles it. We don't have to feel guilty about wiping them out. Not any animal that could have survived that long. Ice age and all."

He looked at me strangely. "Wiping them out? No. Never." The vacant look of the native, as he had so recently demonstrated, appeared in his eyes as he scratched the black stubble of morning beard that had appeared on his chin. "They will survive us. Through any holocaust that comes or that we bring upon ourselves. Yes . . ." he said, slowly returning to the moment. "Eggs," he murmured as he began to dig into the mound.

"How do they mate?" I asked.

"They, male and female, can find one another by smell. When they're in heat they exude a musty odor, either in the water or on the ground, and leave a trail that can be easily followed." He sat back on his heels. "And they can find each other by sound, too.

Once during the mating season I heard a group of males exercising their vocal powers. It was quite an experience."

"What does it sound like?"

"Oh! They bellow, they roar, they howl. At specific intervals. And it's a sound that can carry for considerable distances."

"I wouldn't want to be around then."

"They wouldn't bother you." He smiled at me. "They have other things on their mind at that point."

He returned to the subject of the nest. "Now, once the female is fertilized, she sweeps up a mass of leaves like these and deposits the eggs in the center of the pile and covers them up. Incubation occurs mainly by the heat of this vegetation decaying."

"Does the mother stay nearby?"

"Only when the eggs are ready to hatch, which takes about forty days. But this mound is new. The eggs recently laid. Don't worry." He dug deeper into the mound and pulled aside some more leaves revealing about twenty more eggs. "They can lay up to ninety."

"I feel the mother's watching us. Let's go," I said, rising to my feet and backing away.

"Don't worry, I say," Henri assured me, recovering the mound. "She only hangs around the nest when she knows the eggs are about ready to hatch. Listens for the telltale noise of the scratching of their 'egg tooth' against the side of the shell, breaking through. Did you know this tooth is only for that purpose? And they lose it once they have broken through. Then, once the mother hears their hiccough-like cries among the leaves, she scratches away the covering of the nest. The hatchlings are two or three times the size of the eggs from which they emerge and even before they are completely out of the shell their tiny jaws are powerful enough to bite your finger off. They are born ready to fend for themselves. All the mother crocodile has to do is lead them to the water."

We heard the sound of someone or something running down the path, coming towards us. Henri's hand went automatically to his pistol in the holster slung around his waist. We couldn't tell if it was a person or an animal.

It was Oscar. He burst through the underbrush and into the clearing, visibly agitated. Something extraordinary had happened to the unshakable Oscar. He cried out in alarm and Henri turned me around. "Let's go!"

We hurried back to the shore without another word. Once there, Henri huddled together with Oscar and Gabriel, the two of them gesticulating furiously. Henri listened carefully. Then he came over to Jean and me and announced, "We'll have to pack up. They won't stay another minute."

Gabriel doused the fire and I handed out the fried bacon, which everyone quickly devoured, then rinsed the pan out in the river. The crocodile eggs were left on the shore. Within minutes we were back in the overloaded pirogue and headed out toward the middle of the shallow river where the current was swift.

"What happened?" I shouted to Henri above the roar of the approaching falls. I sat on my taboret, my feet resting on the gavial's tail. Gabriel, behind me, sat on the pile of smaller crocodiles.

"Oscar found the village that was once invaded by migrating crocodiles."

I waited. Henri was standing up, watching the river carefully. Ahead, to starboard, was a wooded island where the river separated into two parts and where large, menacing rocks were sticking out of the water offshore of this island. Jean stood up, too. We headed back against the current towards the shore to avoid them.

"What does that mean? Invaded by crocodiles?" Henri remained standing, legs astride the head of the gavial, eyes on the river. He didn't appear to have heard me. "Shallow. Too shallow," he replied. "The rainy season was a dry one this year and now its effects are showing up. We could be in for a bad drought. Don't expect the rainy season for three more months and, in the meantime, the river could dry up. When that happens the crocodiles hibernate in mud holes. And when they dry up . . . . It could happen again . . . . "

"What?"

Still without taking his eyes off the river, he shouted back, "An invasion! That village was once invaded by hundreds of crocodiles looking for water. They came out of their dried-up mud holes and ran overland, passing through that village in the night. They took the people in their sleep. They ran right through their huts, destroying many of them, ate sleeping babies on their way, tearing off the arms of the women as they tried to defend their children and grabbing the legs of the men as they tried to run away."

"*My God.*" *It was my nightmare.* For a moment I wondered if those bad dreams I had, had not been for a purpose. Couldn't dreams serve as premonitions, warnings of things to come?

"Crocodiles can run fast on land, I assure you," Henri continued. "They can run as fast as a horse for fifty meters anyway. That's in a straight line, of course. When angry enough, or frightened enough, if they want to they can certainly outdistance a man, even zigzagging."

"Where were they going?" I asked.

"To the water below the falls. Nothing but cataracts and then rapids there but they can navigate them until they come to where the river deepens and opens up again."

"Do such migrating herds ever come back?"

"I've never heard of it. Here they would have a hard time climbing back up these cliffs. But the people deserted their village anyway and never came back. It's considered cursed. Even though Oscar and Gabriel aren't superstitious, they weren't about to stay to challenge the spirits that are said to hover about that place."

We were flying along now, for the river was narrowing, and its current increasing with every yard. The roar of the falls was coming closer. The wind could not reach us there between the cliffs and the surface of the fast-moving dark water was smooth and sleek like engine oil dumped in a creek. But here and there were ominous furrows and ripples betraying the hidden inequalities of the riverbed.

A grayish, purple mist hung over the cliffs and, when they diminished in size, the rushing water became clear, glassy green. Henri decided he had gone as far as he dared to go in the shallow water without scraping bottom and damaging the motor. Jean, under his direction, headed us toward a sandy beach in the shelter of a large rock outcropping, around which the water had pooled sufficiently to tie up the overloaded pirogue.

"We can continue along the shoreline on foot," Henri said, taking my hand, helping me out of the canoe. "The falls are only about sixty meters up ahead."

We walked along in single file, stepping from one half-submerged rock to another, Henri leading, me close behind, Jean following me and then Oscar and Gabriel taking up the rear. Jean broke off an over-hanging branch for me to use as a walking stick and as a probe to test the surface of the river under my feet. It helped me, somewhat, to gain confidence in my footing, but mostly I just followed Henri, as best I could, for he walked very rapidly, and I had a hard time keeping him in sight. Soon the riverbed rocks merged into a single flat shelf of slate, which enabled us to walk toward the roar of the falls as easily as if we were walking on a flooded sidewalk.

When we could go no farther, we climbed up onto the shore and from an overhanging boulder looked down into the depths of the cauldron hundreds of feet below, where the roiling waters of the Kwango had been transformed into mist and foam. The steamy spray produced by the power of this phenomenal force of nature drenched us thoroughly and its thunder sent shivers of excitement through me greater than I had ever experienced, including the roar of the crowd at midnight on New Year's eve in Times Square.

There were four beautiful rainbows arcing so low in the sky above this spectacular sight that I felt I could practically reach out and grab one for my very own.

View of the Guillaume Falls.

# 10.

## THE VILLAGE OF THE DEAD

"NOW, FOR THE rest of my life," I told Henri, "every time I see a crocodile handbag or pair of shoes for sale anywhere in the world, I will be back here on the Kwango, in the village Tansuni."

Henri nodded, without looking up. He was sitting on the back of the great gavial, helping to separate the animal from its skin. He worked with loving care as he caressed the beast with his knife. His eyes shone. It occurred to me that he had—that there existed in some part of him—a love-hate relationship with his crocodiles, in the sense that they were objects to be pursued, seduced and conquered. I had by now realized that real hunters, like Henri, are true animal lovers, even crocodile hunters. But during the hunt he was more than that. He was infatuated to the point of obsession with the crocodiles he sought out. Nothing much in the world existed for him but their seduction and conquest.

End of 2nd hunt. Author triumphant sitting atop giant
gavial crocodile.

Night's catch 2<sup>nd</sup> hunt. Pirogue in foreground.

Author with rookie hunter Jean Lauwerens seated on giant gavial crocodile.

"Have you heard from that French company you were interested in?"

"No."

At that moment a great commotion was heard in the village. "Bwana! *Bwana*," people called out to Henri. Four men staggered down to the beach bearing a large black gorilla on a makeshift stretcher. Women, children and the men who had been tending the smoking crocodile meat fires followed. Even Chief Makuba appeared.

The men set the stretcher down and rolled the gorilla onto the ground. Then they pulled him up into a sitting position. The gorilla's eyes were open, looking at us. At first, I thought he was alive and wanted to run away but no one else moved. His mouth was wide open, too. Jaws apart. Why wasn't he moving? I wondered. Why was he just staring at us with suffering eyes? Eyes that had seen something terrible. Why was his mouth open as though frozen in the act of howling with fury? Or pain. Then, in the next instant, I noticed the gunshot hole over his heart, out of which trickled a telltale rivulet of blood. The gorilla was dead.

Henri approached him, listening to the story of the men who had brought him in. "These men," Henri translated for me, and then for Jean, "were tracking a hunting party nearby. Two white men had caught a female baby gorilla in a trap. And as they were loading her into their truck, this male, hearing her cries for help, came to her rescue. They shot him and left him there."

I felt sick. Revolted. Appalled.

"Filthy zoo hunters!" Henri spat out with infinite disgust. "I wonder if they had a license. Probably not. The men tell me they headed for the Angolan border. I wonder what's going to happen after independence? The place will be crawling with zoo hunters, that's what. It's a very lucrative business, you know."

"What can you do?"

"Nothing. Nothing. But I'll report it to the territorial administrator when we get back."

Gorilla killed while defending his child from poachers.

Then he asked Jean to hand him the tape measure he was using to measure the crocodiles. To me he said, "Please take down the measurements in your little book as I call them out. The authorities must have an idea of the size, in case they have been tracking him. And I'm sure they have. I'm sure they know who he is, because he's an old fellow and must have been around this area for a long time. I imagine those poachers killed the patriarch of the entire territory."

According to the measurements Henri gave me, translated into feet, the gorilla was six and a half feet tall, arms three and one-fourth feet long, and his legs three feet. The arm span from the tip of one hand to the tip of the other was an incredible seven and a fourth feet. He was as big as the one I had seen Claude give a cigarette to in the Leopoldville zoo. The one who had looked at me as though he knew me.

When Henri had finished taking the gorilla's measurements, the men laid him back on the stretcher they had carried him in on. I bent over him and closed his anguished eyes, trying not to look too long into their depths for fear they would haunt me always. I could do nothing about the mouth. It remained open.

"What will they do with him now?" I asked. But before he had a chance to reply I added, "No. Don't tell me. I really don't want to know."

Henri sighed. "They will give him a decent burial, I suspect. So his spirit can join those of the other spirits of his kind who have gone to live in the village of the dead."

It was almost two o'clock by the time the skins were salted and packed into the jeep and we were ready to head back to Leopoldville. Near Kabuba we stopped by the stream Gambo for our much-needed dip to wash the grime from our sleep-deprived bodies. This was followed by our picnic. Jean made the fire for our stew pot and Henri added the crocodile meat, a chunk of crocodile fat, the tomato paste diluted with a bottle of burgundy, the onions and finally a dash of pili-pili.

"Can you eat all parts of the crocodile?" Jean asked Henri, carefully setting the fat aside.

"Everything except the brains. They are poisonous. But," he looked at the fat on Jean's tin plate, "the fat will protect you from all poisons."

With that Jean did not hesitate to swallow his portion slowly, carefully, as one would a magical antidote. And so did I.

There was a soft red glow on the horizon where the sun was setting when I asked, "What does that mean, Henri, the *village of the dead?*"

It was cognac time now and we were all feeling mellow. Henri poured himself some more and began, "It's part of their religion. You see, to begin with, contrary to what a lot of people think, the Congolese do believe in God. In a Supreme Being. He's at the top of the hierarchy of beings and communicates His strength, His might, His creative force and, in some cases, His goodness to them. The Bayaka people here, for instance, have at least six names for God that I know of, like the Being Par Excellence, the Spirit Par Excellence, the Architect, the Creator of the Ancestors, He who commands, He who feeds the world."

"Those are wonderful images."

"I think so, too."

"And this village of the dead?" asked Jean.

"*Oui.* You see, they believe that in the bodies of *all* living creatures, human and animal alike—even the trees in the forest, the fish in the river—is a vital force. The higher you go up the evolutionary ladder, the greater the force. And man, being at the top of the scale, has the greatest amount of this force or energy. At death something definitely disappears and returns to the Supreme Force, *but an element continues to live on,* generally in what they refer to as the village of the dead."

Jean and I thought about this for a while as we slowly sipped our cognac, while the darkness was falling about us.

"This part that disappears," I finally said, "is that what we would call the soul?"

"If you wish .... Many tribes also believe," Henri continued, "that what survives, what lives in the village of the dead, can be reincarnated in either another human being or an animal."

"Such as a gorilla?"

"Most definitely."

I shuddered, for I could still see that slain gorilla's eyes staring at me in infinite pain. "He looked so human," I said. "And the crocodile, too, I suppose?"

"For some tribes, yes."

And then I added, "I suppose the Congolese feel that the forest belongs to them. The river, the savannah and that we are trespassing."

"Of course. According to native law, individual land ownership does not exist. There is only collective land ownership. The land belongs to the clan, which is a community made up of family groups consisting of *all* the descendants—living and dead—of a common ancestor and, in theory, all the generations to come. It's part of their religion."

"And somewhere on each community's land lies their village of the dead?"

"Yes. And the spirits that live there may become unhappy either because their descendants have ceased to honor them or because the family has died out. Hell for them is when a clan dies out and the ancestors in the village of the dead are abandoned."

"And they are no longer remembered," I concluded. "Hell, then," I mused, "is when you die and no one remembers you anymore."

"You could say that."

"Your spirit, though, is okay, lives on, as long as you are remembered. Is that it?"

Henri nodded.

Some minutes later I asked him, "So they can never sell their land?"

"No. It belongs at one and the same time to the living, the

dead and the unborn. The right to make use of it, though, can be granted to strangers but only by a special member of the clan who has been given this authority by the ancestors. He's called the *chef du terre*, the land chief."

"And you have been given this right by the people of Tansuni?"

"Yes. For the hut and the garden that goes with it. And for the right to hunt on the river. But not to own. That's impossible. Just to make use of and only for as long as this land chief wishes. Call it a concession, if you wish. And no concession is ever looked upon as perpetual."

"The plantations?" asked Jean.

"They are only concessions. Negotiated concessions. Though things are changing in the cities and natives are insisting on owning their own private property."

"I wonder if, after independence and a new government, the people will want their old concessions back? What will happen to companies like," I turned to Jean, "your Unilever?"

"That's a very good question," Henri replied. "The Belgian government doesn't seem to realize the importance of the concept of the clan. Or has forgotten."

"Nothing changes for Unilever," declared Jean. "The president promised before I left Brussels."

Henri laughed. "What does he know?"

It was midnight by the time we reached Leopoldville. After dropping Jean off at the Hotel Memling, where he was staying until taking up his post in the Kasai, Henri helped me carry my things up to my apartment.

"I like the idea of having a village of the dead, don't you?" I asked, opening my door. "A place where a part of you, your spirit, lives on as long as someone remembers you?"

"It's comforting."

"It doesn't make death seem so brutal, so final, as it is in our culture. We are not so very smart, are we?"

His reply was to ask, "You can come again?"

"I would like that."

Before getting into the elevator he turned around and said in a grave tone, like a man who has reached an important decision, "Let me know when you are ready."

# 11.

## THE SHADOW WORLD

I T WAS 2 P.M. the following Sunday and the broad Boulevard Albert was deserted. Everyone was either still eating lunch or taking their siesta. I was tired and had excused myself early from the farewell party being given by the economics officer for Bill Hart. But I was not so tired as I drove home that I couldn't marvel, as I did every afternoon, at the dramatic array of cumulus clouds, piling up as high as a nearby mountain range on the edge of the blue horizon. As I automatically signaled my left-hand turn into the crossover lane between the two directions of traffic, I spied a little red sports car in my rearview mirror coming up fast behind me. I thought nothing of it. The car had two empty lanes in which to pass me as I moved into the crossover lane. But he hadn't seen me. He caught the rear end of my sedan sticking out of the crossover lane and sailed right through the air over the top of my car. This impact spun me around in the opposite direction from which I had been coming and pushed me up onto the grassy island separating the four lanes of traffic.

I staggered out and looked over at the smoking and crumpled car, crushed like a toy under foot. It had flipped over and landed upside down in the deep ditch on the other side of the Boulevard. It was an MG, like Claude's, only it was red. A young man climbed out of the passenger side and collapsed into the ditch. A few people appeared on the balconies of the apartment buildings lining the other side of the Boulevard. Within minutes the police were alongside me.

"*My God. My God, not again!*" screamed my brain as I held out my diplomatic passport, which the police ignored, and attempted to answer their bewildering questions, such as "Father's name? Address? His place and date of birth? Mother's name? Address? Her place and date of birth?" I couldn't remember. I had no idea what this meant. Was I dreaming? Why were they asking me these questions? All I could reply was, "I signaled! I signaled! Why couldn't he have seen me! There was no one else!"

I started to run over to the MG but the police grabbed my arm saying, "Don't. The driver is dead."

I felt my legs going out from under me but a policeman held me up, saving me from falling to the pavement. "An ambulance is on its way for the passenger," another policeman said, "You'll have to come to headquarters with us."

Another man's voice behind me called out in a supremely authoritative manner, "Leave her alone! Haven't you taken notice of her diplomatic plates? You can contact the United States Consulate tomorrow. They can answer your questions."

I turned to this voice and saw it belonged to an older man, massively built. The policemen snapped to attention. "Yes, Captain!"

This stranger, with the body of a retired wrestler, then put his arm around my shaking shoulders. "My God!" I sobbed against his chest. "There was no one. No one here. The Boulevard was empty. And I wasn't even on the Boulevard! *Why couldn't he have seen me?*"

"Perhaps," the man gently replied, "he wasn't looking." Then he asked, "Shall I take you to the hospital?"

"No." I began to cry in earnest. "Please just take me home." I had shed no tears after my accident in Cairo but now they wouldn't stop. "All I want to do is go home. *Please. Please. Please.* Just take me home."

"Are you sure? Are you all right?"

It was only then that I felt my neck hurting from the whiplash I had suffered when my car had spun around. "Maybe it's just my neck," I replied. He continued to stare at my face. I felt my left cheek where my robin's egg of a blood clot was still visible and replied, "This comes from before. From another accident. In Cairo."

The man nodded slowly and continued to stare.

"I live just down the street. I was only making the turn to go home when—"

"It's all right. Just come with me. I'll take you home. The police will follow with your car."

He led me to his big black Buick and I got in. By now a crowd had gathered. Departing guests from Bill Hart's party and other consulate members had come upon the scene. "I'm all right," I assured Hart, as his wife Celeste and his three little boys looked on, wide-eyed. "I just want to go home."

He hesitated. "That this has to happen to you! So soon after Cairo!"

"I'll see that she is taken care of," the stranger that the police called "Captain" told him.

"All right," Hart, grim-faced, agreed. "I'll call later and check. And," he looked over at the waiting policemen, "I'll take care of them."

The Captain turned the air-conditioning up high, pulled down the covers of my bed, helped me to stretch out, and brought extra cushions from the living room couch to put under my neck. Then he emptied the ice trays in the refrigerator, wrapped them in towels from the bathroom and fitted them around the back of my neck. "Try not to move," he said. Soon he appeared with a tumbler of Scotch from the supply he found in the kitchen. No more than a sip passed my lips before I passed out.

When I awoke he was sitting by the side of the bed, holding my hand and gently stroking my forehead, murmuring, *"Mais comme tu es belle . . . ."*

In his mid-fifties, this man wore thick glasses. His eyes, large and chocolate brown set in his wide, round, Buddha-like face looked down on me, radiating compassion.

"Who are you?" I asked.

"Jens. *Maurice Jens.*" He pronounced his name, sharply, crisply, as though he was snapping to attention before an invisible commanding officer.

"Captain?"

"Yes."

I waited.

"Captain of the Congo. Director of OTRACO. Otherwise known as *l'Office d'Exploitation des Transports Coloniaux.*"

"I've heard of it. Isn't that the government agency that manages the steamships and barges?"

"And the inland waterway system. I run a small army of captains, pilots and crews, agents, clerks. For the moment I have thirty-five steamships under my command," he said, removing the melting ice pack from around my neck. "But," he smiled briefly for the first time and with a hint of cynicism in his voice told me, "despite all that you have nothing to fear from me." Then he straightened up and left the room.

Indeed, Captain Jens carried his considerable bulk with the dignity of a commanding general. He returned from the kitchen with another tumbler of Scotch, this time diluted with soda water, and a pill, "To help you sleep."

I sipped my drink slowly. "Please help yourself as well," I urged.

He did so and we drank together in silence. His eyes clouded over as he stared at me, as though he was seeing not me but someone else, remembering something that had happened long ago. It was the look, it seemed to me then, of a military officer who had seen many campaigns and waged many battles with both men and nature. I soon drifted off to sleep, confident that the man watching over me was a friend.

The merciless morning sunlight streaming in my bedroom window stabbed at my closed eyes and I awoke to find the Captain still sitting by my bedside.

"I've been watching over you all night," he smiled. "How is your neck?"

I sat up and turned it slowly from side to side. "Fine. Just fine."

"Let me see."

I rolled over onto my stomach and allowed him to examine and then briefly massage the tendons.

The front door opened. It was Jean-Pierre. "I can go now," Jens announced. "Your houseboy has just arrived. But I shall check in on you this evening."

Bill Hart called to report that everything had been arranged with the police and I wouldn't be needed at headquarters. "Just stay put and get some rest. The passenger testified that indeed he saw you signal. He tried to warn his friend but it was too late. He thought he was all alone on the road."

As I lay back on my pillows, I wondered if perhaps the driver hadn't also been looking at the clouds, as I had been. Except he had kept on going. Right into them. I hoped he would forgive me. I promised myself that I would never forget him. Though I had not seen his face, he would be remembered in the village of the dead that we call a cemetery.

Captain Jens knocked at my door that evening, holding in his hand a beautifully polished bronze kerosene ship's lantern. "For you," he said. "From your country. I want you to have it, a souvenir from this country given back to its rightful owner. How are you?"

"I'm okay. Still a bit shaky but as the doctor in Cairo said, I must have rubber bones. What do you mean?" I looked at the lantern he had placed in my hand. "From my country?"

"Turn it over and you will see."

It read, "Made in Brooklyn. 1876."

We sat on my balcony, he with a Scotch and soda and I with an orange juice, flavored with rum, watching the sun set over the

Congo as the lights of Brazzaville came on across the way like premature stars in the firmament.

"That lamp," he began to explain, "comes from my first command thirty-five years ago. A ship that came from your country. The Mississippi."

"The *Mississippi?*" I didn't understand.

"Yes. Most of the paddleboats on the Mississippi were decommissioned in the 1920s in favor of oil-fired steamers. Whereas here, fuel was never a problem. And it still isn't. There is plenty of firewood to be purchased along the river for the boilers of these paddleboats. 'Packa-packas' are what the Congolese call them because that is the sound they make as they chug along, huffing and puffing, as each blade of the great paddle wheel dips into the river, propelling it forward, bringing its cargo to Leopoldville. In the past it was ivory, rubber. Now it's coffee, palm oil, copper, *cacao,* lumber, sometimes diamonds and even gold, and since the War, uranium ore."

"How did they ever get them here?"

"They were dismantled piece by piece, loaded onto cargo vessels in New York and shipped across the Atlantic to the port of Matadi at the mouth of the Congo. There, Congolese carried the parts on their backs over the 150 miles of jungle path that followed the rapids until reaching the first navigable part of the river, which is at Leopoldville. The railroad hadn't been built then, of course. And here in Leopoldville they were reassembled. Two are still in use today, thirty-five years later."

"Your first command?" I asked, admiring the golden lantern now balanced on the railing of my balcony as it glittered in the rays of the setting sun.

"Yes. And I'll never forget my first trip on that paddleboat! I was nineteen and came here seeking my fortune. My father was a North Sea pilot, and my grandfather before him, and his father before that. Half the families in Antwerp have one foot in the sea, you know. But the seas my fathers knew were cold and the life hard. I wanted warmer climes. So I came here, full of piss and vinegar. They gave me a paddleboat right off and told me to take it to Coquilhatville, almost 1,000 kilometers from here. I was alone at the helm. No charts. I was terrified," he remembered. "As was my native crew. They knew damn well I didn't know the river!" His voice was grim as he remembered and smiled at me, lifting his glass to his lips.

"You see," he continued, "the Mississippi is much like the Congo and that's why the paddleboats they once used there work well here. Both rivers are shallow in places, deep in others, depending upon the season. Hidden sandbars, capricious currents—sometimes swift, sometimes lazy—and often full of floating debris. Logs and other things washed into the currents from the tributaries, great trees felled by storms. Obstacles that can make navigation hazardous at times."

"I know. I've already seen something of your rivers. The Kwango. I've gone crocodile hunting."

He leaned forward. "I know," he said, with a knowing, Buddha-like grin on his broad face and a twinkle in his eye. "I know who you are."

"The coconut wireless?"

"Not necessary." He leaned back and chuckled. "I have my spies. Everywhere."

"Oh, my . . . Jean-Pierre?"

"Sure. Among others. You really had him worried."

"Do you know Claude Stylo?"

"Naturally. Who wouldn't know the manager of the Banque du Congo Belge? Brussels isn't going to keep him very long in Goma. He's too valuable a man. But they'll probably keep him there until after independence to manage the transition period. Then they'll recall him to Belgium."

"I hope so, for his sake. He hates it here."

"I can well understand why."

"So, you know the story?"

"Everyone does. You're keeping his things for him, aren't you?"

"Some things. But that doesn't mean—"

"I know. I told you I know the man."

"You must know, then, Henri, the crocodile hunter who works at the bank?"

"You mean Soulé? Certainly."

"Soulé? Funny, I never knew his last name."

He sat back in his deck chair, drawing deeply on his Belga cigarette, a brand I had come to appreciate as well.

After a long silence, each one of us thinking our own thoughts, he announced, "I'm *Lord Jim*, you know," he said, speaking not to me but to the twilight. "You have to understand that straight off. And then you will have no need to ask further questions. You know *Lord Jim*, don't you? Conrad?"

"Yes. I do. The officer who abandoned his passengers on his sinking ship, only to save himself on an island where he was made king, but could never go home again."

"Something like that."

Once more we smoked in silence for a long time before he finally spoke again. "Your crocodile hunter, he's another Lord Jim," he said, emptying his glass.

As I took it from him, he looked hard into my eyes through his thick magnifying lenses and added, "But then, the Congo is full of them."

When I returned with another Scotch for him, I told him, timidly, drawing in my breath momentarily, that what I'd really like to do would be to take a trip all the way up the Congo to Stanleyville on one of his steamers. "Something I could write about," I rushed on. "A trip that would live forever in my memory when I leave this place. Do you think that's possible?"

"I understand," he replied. "I could arrange it."

"*Wonderful.* How long would it take?"

"Twelve days. Maybe more, depending upon the cargo and the stops. Seven up and five down."

"I don't know if the consulate will let me off for that long but I'll try. I could fly back."

"Let me know when you're ready."

It was only then that I noticed that he wore a wedding ring.

"Tell me about your wife," I asked. "Does she accompany you on your trips like the other Flemish women do?"

"She's in Belgium. Oh, she spent many years here, too. Yes, often sailing with me. But I sent her back long ago. A white woman can only take so much of life on the river."

"I suppose. Not with children."

"Oh, she could never have children. But in Belgium she can be with her nieces and nephews. And we have a long vacation together for six months every three years when I take my leave. But for me, it's sheer torture. You see," he squinted at the ball of fire sitting on the western horizon preparing for its departure to the other side of the earth, "I need the sun. I've gotten used to the sun of the Congo and I can't live without it. After a month in that country where the sun rarely shines, and when it does, it is so weak, I can't wait to get back here."

"And here? Do you have companionship here?"

"Certainly." A boyish grin played about his wide mouth. "Now and then. Congolese women can be very kind. But you're not supposed to know that." He squeezed my hand, put his cheek up against mine and whispered in my ear. "Let that be our secret just between the two of us." Then he drew away and changed the subject, abruptly asking, "Would you like to be my guest at my retirement party next Saturday?"

"Thank you. It would be an honor."

"Where are we going?" I asked Maurice.

"To the party, of course."

We had entered the African *cité* of Leopoldville and were driving down street after street lined with neat, white-washed, small, square, box-like cement block houses. Row upon row of them with only a small handkerchief-sized patch of parched clay soil in front of each. Some inhabitants had made an attempt to wrest a garden out of this earth still filled with construction rubble but most had not. The sun beat down murderously on the shiny new tin roofs. Living inside one of these boxes during the day I imagined would be like living inside an oven.

"Here?"

"Yes." Looking to the right and left, Maurice commented, "They're certainly making progress. Trying to build as many as they can to show off to the King, the dignitaries, the international press and what not, who will surely be arriving for the Independence Day celebrations."

"They look like cages to me," I said, remembering the reed and bamboo huts of Tansuni where the wind filtered through and caressed the sleeper. Where you could look out and see your own palm trees, listen to the song birds in the forest, hear the rush of a nearby mountain stream, and look up at the pure, unpolluted blue African sky, lavishly strewn with clouds so close you could almost hug them.

"Yes, well, they're better than the filthy, disease-ridden tin shacks most of them are living in now on the other side of the *cité*. No water, no sanitation, heaps of garbage everywhere. Roads so rutted and muddy and bad only a jeep can pass and even then, with much difficulty. But the people keep sneaking in from the provinces by the thousands. There's a ban on allowing any more in but they keep coming, anyway. Mostly at night, despite the guards posted everywhere. You need a pass now to get either in or out."

"I know. Jean-Pierre has to have one and I have to sign it."

"The population of the African *cité* is running somewhere around 350,000. That's a lot up against only 20,000 whites in the European part of town, you know," he said as he came to a halt in front of a large, ramshackle café, where Caribbean music was blaring. "Where did you think the party would be? In the governor's mansion?"

"Well, no, but . . . . " I had dressed for something more formal than an African *cité* café and felt distinctly out of place as I got out of the car and a thousand black eyes looked me over with infinite curiosity. I was wearing my favorite dancing dress with an unusually full skirt of white Egyptian cotton. It was made even more extravagant with the addition of two petticoats underneath, one of taffeta that rustled sweetly when I walked, and one of stiff netting that contributed greatly to the ballooning effect of the skirt when I danced. Then it was transformed into a fully furled sail stirred by a brisk wind. I had worn my party shoes as well: white Italian kid leather high-heel pumps. Maurice was also elegantly dressed in a formal, dark blue, shantung silk suit, sporting a red carnation in his lapel. His black leather shoes were polished so well that they could burn a hole in steel if held up to the sun.

"You see, when they told me they were going to give me a party celebrating my thirty-five years of service in the Congo, I told them I would go only if they would hold it here in the African *cité*. That's where all my friends live," he said as he gave me his arm and escorted me into the café.

I laughed. "I'm not even supposed to be here. Bill Hart warned me that the African *cité* is off limits to consulate personnel now."

"They should have no fear. For you are with me."

The music stopped and a great roar of welcome went up as we entered the café. Hundreds of waiting Congolese rushed forward to shake the Captain's hand and to embrace him. Three-fourths of the crowd were young men in their twenties and early thirties and they all appeared to be in uniform consisting of a white shirt, tie, dark trousers, and round, black-rimmed, eyeglasses. It was the uniform of the Congolese clerk or *évolué*, which was what the Belgians called the men who were on their way up the so-called evolutionary scale of European civilization. It was also the uniform of the mayor of Leopoldville, Joseph Kasavubu, who was there as well to congratulate the Captain. The few women invited to attend wore colorful flowing robes with mounds of the same material piled high on their heads. They did not come forward but remained seated demurely at the tables scattered around the café's large dance floor.

Maurice and I were seated—alone—at a table placed before the band and not far from the center of the dance floor, for all to see and observe. Beer had been flowing before our arrival and now it came out by the caseload, running like the chutes of

*Guillaume* down the throats of the men, as though they had just come from the desert and no amount of liquid could quench their thirst. Large platters of roasted peanuts and other Congolese delicacies, including crispy forest insects and grubs deep-fried in palm oil, were passed around. Maurice helped himself to generous quantities of this food. When I demurred, he urged me to at least try the fried flying ants. "They are delicious," he said, helping himself to a handful. "And expensive. They are only sold by the spoonful. These grubs, too, are a great delicacy. They come from the heart of a palm tree," he explained. But I preferred to stick to the roasted peanuts.

Conversation came to a halt when the mayor mounted the bandstand to speak of Captain Jens and his accomplishments. He spoke in Lingala, the language of the river, and presented him with a beautifully carved ivory statue of a tribal chief, or an African deity, but having the features of a white man, and bearing a close resemblance to Maurice. Then a handsome, distinguished looking young white man with a blond beard came forward. He was wearing an elegantly cut navy blue blazer with white trousers and a silk foulard tucked into the neck of his white dress shirt. He presented Maurice with a plaque from OTRACO commemorating his years of service. After Maurice had thanked all present in Lingala, the celebration continued and the beer flowed once again.

Returning to our table Maurice looked at the statue and shook his head. "It's almost blasphemous. They shouldn't have." He was not pleased. "I am not an African god."

"No," I smiled, turning the statue over in my hand, "but you are obviously a chief for them. How they seem to adore you!"

"Yes. For the moment, anyway."

"Who was the man with the beard?"

"My closest friend here. Captain Dallemagne. You'll meet him one day. He started out as a river pilot just like me and now runs the new School of Navigation here in Leo. But his contract is up and, I imagine, he soon will be taking over his family's plantations."

The ceremonies over, the band played calypso. But no one danced. The large, circular wooden floor laid down over the dirt one of the café remained empty. "They are waiting for us to begin," Maurice said.

I demurred. This was not the village Tansuni and I fresh from the rush and glory of a victorious crocodile hunt. But when the band played "Island in the Sun," I stood up and proffered my hand to the Captain, "May I have this dance?" It was a song from the film of the same name that I had worked on two years before on the island of Grenada. "Island In The Sun" was a film about interracial relationships and had been banned in many southern states in the United States. How odd, I thought, that it be I, for whom politics or race relations had little meaning who would be the one, out of all those socially conscious people who had worked on that film, to witness the first African country south of the Sahara receive its independence. "How odd," I called out, as Maurice expertly propelled me around the otherwise empty dance floor. No one else joined us. The people stood by, watching our performance intently.

"What do you mean?"

"Nothing," I decided as I started to sing the words of the song and the band played on with Maurice whirling, twirling me around the dance floor.

At the song's conclusion, the crowd cheered and stamped their feet in admiration. Now that they knew what I wanted to hear, the band played another tune from the same film: "Lead Man Holler."

By the end of this dance both Maurice and I were sweating from the exertion of our efforts. It was sweltering inside the café not only because of the crowd but as a result of the merciless sun beating down on its tin roof without the benefit of any nearby shade tree. I could feel the back of Maurice's suit jacket wet with his perspiration, yet he refused to take it off. The bodice of my own dress was soaked through with the sweat trickling down my neck and from underneath my arms.

Captain Maurice Jens dancing with Author during his
retirement party.

Soon after we had returned to our table, Maurice decided it was time that we could, without offending our audience, take our leave, "Before we both melt away," he said. "Let's go to my place. It's an old colonial house, but I recently installed air-conditioning and we could cook a couple of steaks. They came in on today's Sabena flight. Chateaubriand from Brussels."

Our leave-taking took a considerable amount of time. There was much shaking of hands and embracing before we were able to get away. Among the well-wishers I recognized Joseph, who was my librarian's assistant and the consulate's eyes and ears in the African *cité*.

Once in the car Maurice said, "Now they can enjoy themselves." The music blared once again out into the street, amplified by loud speakers mounted on the roof of the café. "I gave the manager enough money for beer for half the population of the *cité*."

Maurice's large home was located in the residential part of Leopoldville reserved for Europeans, on the other side of Boulevard Albert from the African *cité*, and along the river. Almost hidden among a grove of mango trees, it was fronted by a lush, carefully tended tropical garden, overflowing with exotic plants and unfamiliar flowers. A circular driveway wound through this small slice of paradise up to the wide Victorian-style veranda of his house.

"I'll go around the back and open the front door for you," he said.

I heard music coming from within as I walked up the porch steps and glimpsed a dark feminine figure—no more than a shadow—behind the curtains. Upon seeing me, she ran to turn off the music and then fled up the stairs. I knew immediately who it must be.

After Maurice had opened the door for me, I said, "You should ask her to join us," I told him, following him into the kitchen.

"No," he refused. "It wouldn't be right."

"But you can't keep her upstairs like that. I couldn't stay

here and eat with you knowing she is hiding. You must ask her to come down."

Again he refused.

"It's a question of dignity. Of honor," I protested.

He hesitated. Then once more refused.

"It's up to you, of course," I said, annoyed, and walked away. When I turned around, he had disappeared. I heard voices upstairs. His pleading. Hers angry. Then both of them walked into the kitchen.

"This is Josephine," Maurice announced. The young woman was cringing with embarrassment as she entered. But then, facing me, her regard was sullen, dark, and her eyes as fierce as a tigress as she looked into mine. She refused to accept my proffered hand. Then she refused to help us cook our steaks. Maurice did not insist, so we grilled them while she stood by watching, stirring a pot of stew she had been cooking, all the while throwing me silent, hateful looks. Tall, slim, with high cheekbones, she had a full, beautifully shaped bosom. Her skin was not polished black like the usual Congolese woman but had a mat-like tone, as though she was wearing makeup. Her features were those of the proud tribes of the northeastern Congo, who had their origins in the Sudan.

She refused to join us in the dining room when our steaks were ready. And I thought to myself, Maurice was right. I was foolish to insist on her presence. In my ignorance I have done nothing but harm to two people.

After we were seated and had begun to eat, Maurice said, "You have had your breath taken away, no? Now you feel strong. You have a big weapon against me." His tone was sarcastic, yet full of pain.

"No," I replied. "It's her I feel sorry for."

"They can be very kind, you know. And I have been lonely."

"I understand. Believe me, I do."

I needed to show him that I did and told him about my latest crocodile hunt, about the gentle and kind people of the village Tansuni, about the poor, brave gorilla and how I had closed its eyes. About the village that had been destroyed by marauding, migrating crocodiles. About what Henri had told me of the native beliefs. About the village of the dead. "I'm beginning to think their beliefs are actually more sophisticated than ours."

He nodded. "Take the pigmies, for instance," he said. "They believe that a human being is made up of three things: the physical body, which disintegrates with death, of course, and disappears. What is left is the soul, and what they call the *megbe*, or one's shadow. The soul after death is carried away to God on the wings of an insect. It's one's *shadow* that lives on in the village of the dead and *where they can get in touch with the living*. There the departed lead a life rather similar to their earthly existence, provided the line of their descendants is maintained."

"I like that idea even better," I smiled. "The shadow world. It's one's shadow that goes on living . . . . "

Later we drank champagne on my apartment balcony looking down on the stars reflected in the Congo River below. They appeared to me to be like luminous drops of life falling from the infinite space above. Maurice said, "Let my affair be our secret, then. The Congo is not ready for such things now."

"Of course. I promised you that once before. 'The Secret Sharer,' I am. Do you know that story by Conrad too?"

"Naturally. It's about the young English captain who concealed a stowaway in his own cabin. A stowaway who had murdered a bully on his ship and who then had jumped overboard in the night to escape being put in chains and returned to England to face the death penalty."

"Yes. That's it. He swam to this other ship in the harbor and came aboard while the young captain was on watch. It was his first command. Somehow he recognized himself in this other young officer and could not bring himself to turn him in."

"Oh," Maurice sighed. "I know that story only too well, because, *ma petite*," his voice dropped to a whisper, "the same thing happened to me. Only my murderer was an Italian, and his sin, a crime of passion, not one of mutiny. I discovered him hiding among the crates on one of my barges, while all of Leopoldville was looking for him. Oh, he's out there somewhere. Somewhere in the bush. I gave him my gun, too, as did the young English captain. Now." He got up from his deck chair and put his hand on my shoulder. "That we've had confession, we can take communion."

I didn't understand.

"Please, let me kiss you."

I lifted up my head and he kissed me softly, gently on the lips. Once. Only once. Then he returned to his chair and reached for my hand. "I know what you are thinking, *ma petite*. No, not again. I suspect you've been hurt before. I promise you won't be hurt again. Not by me, anyway."

First thing Monday morning Bill called me into his office. Before he had a chance to say anything, I spoke first, "Yes, I know, I was in the African *cité* Saturday night. But it was for a good reason—"

"I know. I know. But you must understand the seriousness of the present situation. The terrible implications it could have if something happened to you over there. Brussels and Washington are treading on delicate ground now. From now on and until independence we're holding our breaths that nothing will happen that could jeopardize this transition period. *We do not go into the African cité except on official business.*"

"What could happen to me?"

"For one thing, you could get caught up in another riot and held hostage. Look at what happened to the French. Brazzaville is still licking its wounds from the riots that broke out before you arrived between two tribes over who was going to be the first Prime Minister of the new republic when they get their independence. On the one hand, the French are indignant that anything so barbaric could happen in a land where they had tried so hard to sprinkle the seeds of their civilization. They are sickened to see what might happen the minute their controls are allowed to slacken. They are appalled to be so brutally forced to see that not a bit of the civilization they have tried to plant has taken root. All has been for naught. All their blood, toil, sweat, and tears. Mostly sweat," he paused, smiling for the first time, "for it's very hot in Brazzaville."

Then he became serious again and continued lecturing. "It's painful enough to have to give up a colony created like that but to have those riots *physically* demonstrate that they should never have been here in the first place is even worse. Now that's really heartbreaking and we don't want that to happen here."

"Well, tell me. Exactly what did happen?"

He took a deep breath and sat back. "After the riots the natives ate the dead. And there were over one hundred killed. Officially. But according to eyewitnesses, five hundred is more accurate. And after the trucks came to take away those that were left, the dogs ate, limb by limb, the ones the natives missed."

"Is that true? I mean, is that *really* true? Or not just some Belgian propaganda? I find it hard to believe. Maybe the natives just took the dead away for burial in their villages. How do we know they ate them?"

"That's what Intelligence reports."

"I see. So those were 'The Troubles.'"

"'The Troubles?'"

"Yes. That's what a colon in Brazzaville called them."

"'*Troubles*,' eh? You see, the French won't admit what really happened! Even to themselves. They can't face it. Look at Leopoldville. The Belgians still haven't gotten over the shock that last January 300,000 natives had the *nerve*, were even capable of entertaining the *thought* of rioting against the city's 20,000 whites. 'But we've given them everything!' they cried out in confusion, like children. 'They are better housed and better taken care of than anywhere else on the continent of Africa!'"

"Yes! I hear that all the time. And I try to explain that you can't fill bellies and ignore hearts, minds. If a man's stomach is full, what else does he have to do but think? And what else is there for him to think about here but independence? It's the only thing he doesn't have. *At least*, I tell them, if they had given the

Congolese some education, as the English and French have done in their colonies, they might have some educated leaders by now like they have in Kenya and Uganda, Rhodesia and Tanganyika. They might have a chance of working things out with them, working together with them in the future, making some kind of deal with them like the French are doing in Guinea. And, Bill, do you know what their reply always is? 'But the French have given them nothing! Take those awful huts in Brazzaville that the natives live in. And then look at our beautiful African *cité*!'"

"They haven't, of course," Bill agreed with me, "understood a thing. They've been salving their consciences for so long with their social programs and beautiful *Belge* or African *cité* that it's impossible for them to let this prop go and see anything beyond that."

"I suppose this is not the moment to ask for a leave of absence? Twelve days? Fourteen?"

"To go where? To do what?" he glared at me. "Another crocodile hunt?"

"No." I smiled sweetly. "I'd like to take the trip to Stanleyville by steamer. Captain Jens said he could arrange it."

"Out of the question. You're needed here. My replacement will soon be arriving and he will need all the help he can get. Name's Ed Johnson and he's being transferred from Katmandu, of all places. Probably can't even speak French."

"Katmandu? Poor guy. From the highest snow-covered mountains to the equatorial jungle. He'll fry here. So the answer is no."

"That's right."

# 12.

## CAPTAIN DALLEMAGNE

R IGHT AFTER I left Bill's office I met Maurice Jens's friend in my library. It was the handsome young man with the blond beard, Captain Dallemagne. He spoke English fluently, with a charming accent: part French and part British. He had the most intensely, startling blue eyes I had ever seen. They were the color of the African sky reflected in the waters of a South Sea lagoon.

He had come for a film for his Navigation School students. The Belgian Information Office was closed that day, he explained, and Captain Jens had suggested he pay me a visit. I was delighted for I had just the film for him, which had recently arrived from USIS headquarters in Washington. It was about the new St. Lawrence River Seaway system. After André had checked the film out for him, he returned to my office and said, "Jens tells me you would like to take a steamer to Stanleyville. If you would permit me to be of assistance, I recommend my last command, the *Reine Astrid*. She's the best, the most modern, and I know, of course, her captain. I could make sure you get the very best of the first class cabins."

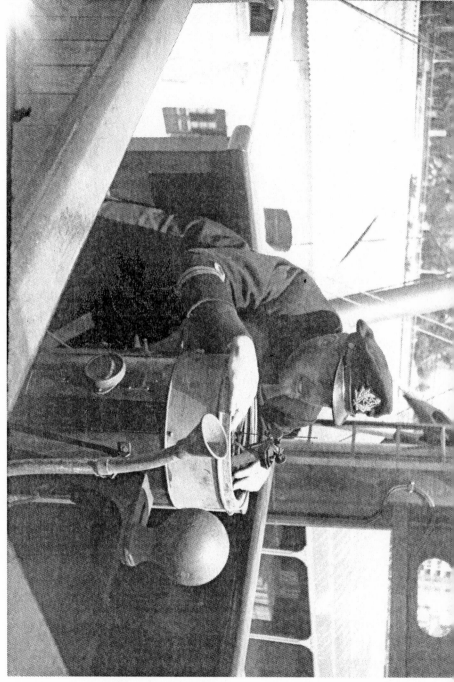

Captain Dallemagne taking a sighting on board one of his Congo River boats.

"Yes," I thanked him, "but it's out of the question for the moment. We're too busy here now and I could never get enough time off to take such a trip."

"Well, then," he replied, "how would you like to take a little ride with me on the river around here? I have an outboard at the yacht club and we could just motor around some afternoon on the Stanley Pool north of here. You'd like it. It's calm. Practically an inland sea where the river broadens before entering the channel for Leopoldville. Surely," he smiled with great charm, "you can spare a few hours for me and the river?"

I had to agree that, yes, I suppose I could. I, who wanted to go the entire length of the Congo, could spare a few hours for the Stanley Pool but I made no definite appointment. So I was surprised when Captain Dallemagne rang my doorbell on Saturday afternoon, asking if I was ready to go.

"But . . . but . . . ," I hesitated. For once I had nothing scheduled for the evening and agreed to the impromptu excursion, asking, "What should I bring?"

"Nothing. Just your bathing suit. We should be back by nightfall."

I quickly changed into a pair of shorts and jersey, wearing my two piece bathing suit underneath, and we set out in his little Renault for the yacht club where Henri also kept his motor boat. Pierre—his name was Pierre—kept his moored a little distance from the club. We parked in the club's parking lot and I shed my shorts and shirt in the car, as he did his, leaving them in the car. Then we both, wearing only our bathing suits, walked through a patch of woods to where Pierre's boat was moored and climbed aboard. It was no bigger than a rowboat or a large dinghy. The air was fresh out on the broad expanse of water known as the Pool. It was so wide that I could not even see the shores of French Equatorial Africa on the north side or barely distinguish the Congo on the south. The breeze on my face, ruffling my hair, was a delicious relief from the stagnant heat of Leopoldville. There were a few sandbanks here and there, a few small islands, and not many water lilies, which Pierre called hyacinths, for us to worry about. There was no other boat in sight. We were alone on the Pool. Absolutely alone. I imagined the relief the first white explorer, Henry Morton Stanley, must have felt when he had come into this wide body of water after emerging from the confines of the upper Congo River, so full of deception and danger at every turn. Being on the Pool was like being on the open sea.

As dusk approached, Pierre turned the little boat around heading back to Leopoldville. Within minutes the motor sputtered and died. "Petrol," Pierre explained, and reached for the Jerry can under his seat. It was attached to the boat by padlock and chain. The can was empty.

"Don't understand!" he fumed. "I filled it yesterday. Believe me." He turned the can upside down. A hole had been punched in the bottom. "*Some bloody thief! Or,*" he added, more softly, almost under his breath, "*sabotage . . .*"

At first I didn't worry. "Someone will come along," he promised. As time passed without another boat or pirogue in sight, I realized we didn't even have a pair of oars. We drifted aimlessly with the current. Pierre tried to paddle the boat with his hands. I had to keep from laughing, thinking how embarrassed he must be. The Captain of the Congo on his first date with me finding himself helpless in the Stanley Pool, so close to Leopoldville and yet so far. We managed, by paddling madly with our hands and feet, to get the boat close enough to a large sandbank, where Pierre leapt overboard, waded ashore and, with the mooring rope, dragged the boat up onto the beach. By this time it was nightfall and our only light was that of a half moon. "We'll have to stay here," he told me. "Can't go on drifting any more or we'll end up in the rapids. We'll wait here until morning for a passing boat. Tomorrow is Sunday and a lot of the yacht club people will be out."

I continued to be amused, thinking what a hilarious mess I had gotten myself into. I was going to spend a night on a sandbank, in the middle of the Congo River, with a man I hardly knew. Both of us were practically naked, with not so much as a towel to cover us and protect us from the chill of the night, nor a morsel of food to stave off our hunger. The only thing Pierre had thought to bring was his tin of English cigarettes and his lighter. Well, I decided, I was no longer the greenhorn from New York. I had been crocodile hunting. I could handle this new challenge. But my amusement and confidence came to a quick halt the minute I set foot on the sandbank. We were attacked by swarms of mosquitoes. Clouds of them engulfed us, flying into our eyes, our ears, our nostrils and our mouths, invading our scalps, swarming around Pierre's beard, biting mercilessly at every exposed piece of skin, which was three-fourths of my body and ninety percent of Pierre's. We hopped up and down like dervish dancers gone crazy, swatting at them trying to escape their onslaught.

"If only we could find some wood, I'd make us a fire and that would keep them away," said Pierre.

We prowled the sandbank, pursued by swarms of our enemy, but in the dark we could only find a few pieces of wet driftwood lying about in the weak moonlight. It was impossible, though, to get a fire started with this wet wood and the feeble spark from Pierre's lighter. Meanwhile, the winged fiends continued to torture us. It was torment to be alive. Remembering Henri's story about being stranded on a sandbank for three days and, as a result, ending up spending three months in the hospital with malaria, I told Pierre, "We can't stay here!"

"No," he agreed. "Let's get back in the boat. Perhaps away from the shore it will be better."

So back in the boat I went, while he got in the river and pulled the boat, the mooring rope over his shoulder, as far away from the sandbank as he could and still stand and control the drifting of the boat. The mosquitoes followed but in somewhat diminishing numbers. I tried to seek shelter by crawling under the one board spanning the narrow boat, which served as the passenger seat, while Pierre dragged the boat, the rope over his shoulder, around and around the sandbank. We had to keep moving. Once still, the enemy attacked anew and with savage vengeance. Despite our suffering, and my anger at Pierre for having gotten me into such a situation, I couldn't help admiring him as he dragged that boat along, just like Humphrey Bogart did for Katherine Hepburn in *The African Queen*. Neither one of us dared voice our concern about the possibility of hungry crocodiles who might be attracted to the movement of Pierre's feet sloughing through the mud and muck of the shallows as he trudged around and around the sandbank.

Around midnight I dozed three or four minutes at a time at the bottom of the boat, huddled under the passenger seat. Once I awoke to see Pierre actually swimming, boat in tow, toward another, much larger, sandbank. When I called out to him, he replied, "Maybe there won't be so many there!" He needed a rest.

But when we got out, it was the same thing. The mosquitoes devoured us in our weakened state. I scraped them off my skin. I spit them out of my mouth and tried to breathe only through my nose but they clogged my nostrils. So it was back into the boat again. I cringed anew under the seat board, arms crossed against my chest, and legs drawn up in a fetal position in my attempt to protect myself from my torturers, while Pierre dragged the boat away from the shore and around and around this sandbank. I felt no nighttime chill as I had on the Kwango, although I was practically naked. The biting insects had warmed my blood to the boiling point.

With the dawn we beached the boat on the sandbank and, exhausted, lay down, arms out-stretched like crucified images on the sandy shore. The few insects that came to bite were almost unnoticeable as compared to the assault we had endured during the night. Around 9 a.m. I awoke under the sledgehammer heat of the sun to the cries of Pierre as he stood in the water attempting to flag down a passing motor launch. Mercifully, the operator and his crew of wife and son saw us and picked us up. They towed our little boat behind them and returned us to Pierre's yacht club mooring. The wife fussed over me, throwing a towel around my sunburned body, swollen with mosquito bites, but I didn't hear what she had to say. I was numb.

Incredibly, Pierre asked that I wait for him in the woods by his boat dock while he went and got the car in the yacht club parking lot. He would meet me in the woods. "You mustn't be seen with me," he explained.

"Why not?" I had suddenly found my voice.

"They will know that we had stayed out all night together."

"So?"

"It's your reputation I'm thinking of. You see, I'm known as something of a ladies man around here." He was serious, his voice grave, almost grim.

"Reputation? *Reputation*! You almost killed me and now you worry about my reputation!" It was so ludicrous a thought that I burst out laughing. But still I waited in the woods, as he asked, for his Renault to appear, which it shortly did. Once inside, I gratefully pulled on my shorts and jersey and said, "Take me home. Don't say another word. Just take me home."

At my apartment door he attempted to apologize, saying perhaps I should see a doctor but I cut him short. All I wanted to do was take a cold shower, cover my poor burned body with cream and sleep forever.

I awoke at 4 p.m. feeling refreshed and hungry. The burning of my skin had subsided, and, though clearly visible, the throbbing of the insect bites had disappeared. At 5 p.m. the doorbell rang. It was Pierre holding a bottle of pills in his hand. "It's for malaria. You will need it."

"Oh, no, I won't! I've taken enough of that stuff to last me a lifetime. Come," I invited him in, suddenly feeling ashamed of the way I had treated him. The loss of petrol hadn't been his fault and it was he who had saved us by dragging that boat around from sandbank to sandbank throughout the night. "Let's celebrate," I suggested. "Let's have a drink."

He called the consulate every morning the following week asking for a lunch date but I assured him I was too busy. What's more, he appeared at my apartment door every evening, content to just, "Check in on you," he said. "See if you are okay," he would explain, as I breezed past him on my way to one reception or another, English classes, or the weekly film showing. On

Thursday he asked, "Would you like to join me on an inspection trip I need to take this weekend? Nothing to do with OTRACO. There's a *cacao* plantation my father has an interest in north of here. A friend of mine who lives in Coquilhatville owns it and wants to sell. If we can buy it, I plan on taking over my father's ranch in the Province Orientale once my contract with OTRACO expires next month. My father would then manage the *cacao* plantation, while I run the ranch. It's becoming too much for someone his age."

"Cocoa . . . ." I was interested. "I'd love to see how it grows," I replied. "I saw some cocoa plantations in Samoa last year. It would be interesting to see how it grows in Africa."

"Good!" His face brightened with the relief of a man who has just received a reprieve from a jail sentence. I couldn't help but feel sorry for him. "I'll come by Saturday morning, 8 a.m., and we'll go," he decided, eyes shining. It's up the Congo north of Bolobo near a village called N'Kolo. About four hundred kilometers from here so plan on staying overnight. There's a shack there we can share. Not much of a place but it's a roof over our heads and with two bunks. And don't worry. I'm a gentleman, I can assure you. Despite my reputation!" he laughed. "And don't worry about food, either. I'll bring everything."

"Just make sure you bring enough extra gas for your car!" I laughed.

He winced under the blow of my sarcasm, bowed his head and assured me, "You can count on that as well."

His Renault held the road well, taking the bumps, ruts, and stray rocks in its stride like an creature familiar with its terrain. It didn't bounce all over the place as had Henri's jeep on the same road.

"Not much *cacao* in the Congo," he told me, "as compared to other countries in Africa like the Gold Coast or Senegal. Conditions are favorable only in the area between Bolobo and Coquilhatville along the river. But what we produce is excellent."

Later, when we stopped by a stream to refresh ourselves, he

opened a tin of foie gras that we spread on crunchy slices of French bread. This appetizer was followed by pieces of tasty cold roasted pheasant and a cucumber salad, accompanied by a bottle of Chablis. For dessert he presented me with a delicious salad of various tropical fruits, including, to my surprise, strawberries. "From the Kivu," he explained. "Flown in yesterday by Sabena. They also grow all year long in the highlands where we have our ranch."

"Where are they exactly? These highlands of yours?"

"Completely on the other side of the Congo, in the northeast, near the Uganda border. They are part of the Ruwenzori Mountain range, also known as the Mountains of the Moon."

"Mountains of the Moon . . . ," I murmured, sipping my wine, "that sounds nice."

"They are. I hope I can show them to you one day," he said, reaching for my hand, and pressing it against his lips, his eyes wide, looking deeply into mine, expecting a response.

But I withdrew my hand gracefully and stood up. "Perhaps. One day when I get enough vacation."

When we reached the point where the Kasai River emptied into the Congo, he pointed out, "It's on the Kasai that you can enter the upper Kwango by paddle steamer. Even with a barge but only in the rainy season when the river is high. I know the Kwango well, have charted it and spent a good deal of time exploring its banks in my motor launch."

Then he glanced at me, eyes narrowing. "I don't think you should continue with your crocodile hunting," he said, pronouncing each word carefully, distinctly, as you would do when speaking to a child. "It's too dangerous."

"Not as dangerous as pleasure boating on the Stanley Pool," I retorted.

He accepted this with grace, smiled, nodded, and changed the subject. "My friend Costermans started this *cacao* plantation about eight years ago and four years ago it started to produce. You'll see," he promised.

We reached the plantation in late afternoon, drawing to a

halt before a wooden shack in a little clearing on a hilltop. Below us flowed the Congo, lazily making its way around jungle islands scattered about in the stream. Beyond lay endless lush green hills. Sensuality trapped, it occurred to me, between the earth and the blue sky, the clouds and the invisible stars. The peculiar musty, pungent odor of the river, teaming with life, was wafted up to me on the sweetest of breezes that played with my hair and cooled my skin.

"I'll show you a place where you can wash," Pierre told me. "While you do so, I'll start a fire for our supper. And then I'll wash, too. Farther upstream. Don't worry. You'll be all alone. No one will see you. You can swim about naked if you wish but stay close to the shore. Tomorrow we'll make an inspection tour with the foreman. He lives in N'Kolo not far away."

Pierre left me by the side of a stream that was rushing through the jungle underbrush towards a waterfall far below. I couldn't see it but I could hear it, and feel its spray, as I sat down on a rock jutting out into the brown and white water rushing to its rendezvous with the ridge ahead and the falls below. There was no need for me to remove my clothes. Within minutes I was thoroughly drenched and cooled off.

Above me, massive branches of trees stretched out over the shoreline. But the leaves of these trees were dusty, not touched at all by the spray of the roaring waterfall. How odd, I mused, to be so close to greatness and not even to feel its touch.

The sun was swiftly setting, for we were not far from the Equator. Yet I didn't want to move from my rock. Suddenly, though, I became frightened of the dangers that might be lurking all around me in the fast-approaching darkness. My heart started to pound and I longed to race back through the small section of forest that separated me from the security of Pierre's company. But I couldn't move. I turned all around and felt the presence of many secret things pressing against me. I was as scared as the child I once was who would lie in her bed, facing the attic door in her bedroom, waiting in terror for the moment when it would open and the monsters who lived up there would come down to devour her.

Then I saw a fisherman and a sense of security descended upon my child's heart once more. He was going home with his catch. Otherwise naked except for a piece of loincloth, he had twelve small fish strung around his waist on a piece of palm fiber. In one hand he clutched a bunch of mushrooms and some shiny green leaves in the other. As he walked across the stream from one half-submerged rock to another, the fish shone silver against his blackness and bobbed up and down, like a ballerina's skirt dancing gracefully in the breeze. He didn't even glance at me. It was as though I had as much right to be there as he did. As if it was perfectly natural and normal that I be sitting there on that rock getting drenched by the spray coming from the falls below.

Pierre had secured two of these fish from this boy, or from another fisherman, and was frying them for us when I returned. The meal was complete with more buttered, crusty French bread, cheese and another bottle of Chablis. By the time the meal was over my clothes were dry. Pierre lit a kerosene lantern and we smoked our cigarettes by the fire's side. He smoked bland, blond, English ones, made from Virginia tobacco. I preferred the strong black Belgas produced in the Congo. We smoked for a long time in silence, listening to the chorus, rather the veritable orchestra, of the creatures of Congo nightlife tuning up all around us.

There had been silence in the middle of the Kwango River. The din had been in the distance, deep in the surrounding forest. But here I was surrounded by a cacophony of sounds, chatter, screeches and buzzing as though I had my ear up against the soundtrack of a Tarzan movie, punctuated now and then by the scream of an animal either in agony or ecstasy. Each time this happened I would jump. "Only a baboon," Pierre assured me. "Individually, they're harmless. But in gangs they can be dangerous."

"Do you have a gun?"

"No. I never carry one. Except on board ship. A Captain must always have a handgun ready. Just in case. But here, I know this country only too well. If you know the country like I do, and the people, you don't need a gun."

He got up and squatted by the edge of the fire, lighting another cigarette with the end of a glowing ember. I went to join him. "Why does your friend want to sell this place? I mean, he can't really sell it, can he? I understand the land belongs to the Congolese and the best you can do is get a concession from the local tribe."

"That's right. It took him five years of negotiations but he got it. And can pass it on, with the approval, of course, of the *chef du terre*. He's the one in charge of such things in the tribe."

"I know."

Then I wondered, "Why does he want to sell now?"

"He doesn't. It's his wife. She's scared she'll lose her servants once independence comes. They have six children and she can't live here without servants. She wants to return to Belgium."

"What do you think will happen after independence?"

"Oh, there will be changes. Some for the better, some for the worse, maybe. But changes there will be and everyone will have to adjust to the new ways. The Congolese as well as the Europeans. Africa cannot isolate itself for long from the rest of the world. The world simply won't let it."

"I agree," I said. "But it will take time."

"Sure. Time. It will take time and I plan to see it, watch it, bear witness to it. My place is here. Europe holds no allure for me anymore."

"Were you in the War?"

"Royal Navy."

"So that's where your British accent comes from."

"Yes. I escaped from Belgium at sixteen, lied about my age and joined the Belgian contingent of the Royal Navy."

"Did you see any action? At such a young age?"

"Certainly. At first, in the North Sea. I was on an MTB boat picking up downed flyers who didn't quite make it back to England after bombing raids over Berlin. It was cold. Oh, so cold . . . . I often felt I would never be warm again. That's one of the reasons I came here."

"I can understand."

"Then," he continued, "there was Normandy, the Battle of the Bulge, the Ardennes Forest. No. Europe is finished for me. The future is here. In Africa." Then ever so casually he asked, "How would you feel about living here?"

"Oh, I wouldn't mind," I replied equally offhandedly.

"But not here." He was emphatic. "You'd be better off in the highlands. Not in the forest. There, in the highlands, the climate is much more suitable for a European."

There were two narrow bunks in the one-room cabin, each furnished with a thin slice of foam rubber. "I'll take the upper one?" I asked.

"Fine," he agreed. "I prefer sleeping closer to the ground."

I climbed up, fully dressed, and covered myself with the rough army blanket Pierre gave me. A few hours later, around midnight, I awoke to the sound of thunder at close range and the whole shack shook back and forth like a box held in the hands of a giant trying to empty out its contents. I held onto to the sides of my bunk, still not fully awake. Surely, I reasoned, I was having one of my nightmares. But it happened again and again. Something was attacking the side of the shack, causing it to tremble ominously. I sat up and screamed. *My God, what's that?"*

Pierre replied from below, his voice soft and reassuring, "It's only a big, old elephant. He's trying to get at the water in the rain barrel. Don't be afraid. There's a rogue one hanging around this part of the forest. He'll go away once he's gotten what he wants. Go back to sleep."

The shack shook violently once again.

"But he'll tear the place down! And trample us to death!"

"Come, then, into my arms, and we shall perish together."

I couldn't tell if he was joking. And I didn't wait to find out. I leapt to the floor and into his arms. He held me tightly against him as the terrible noise in the night continued and our cabin rocked violently from side to side like a small ship caught in an impossible storm. I couldn't decide if I should attempt to escape from the attacking elephant. Get up and run away out into the night. Or if I should continue to cling to Pierre who, I reasoned, had gone mad and didn't care if he lived or died.

But then, just as suddenly as it had begun, the attack ceased. I held my breath in the ensuing silence. "He's got what he came for," Pierre whispered in my ear. Then we heard the rumbling sound of what could have been a tank moving off, going away back into the forest. "He's gone. Now you can return to your bunk, so we can both get some more sleep. It's going to be a long day tomorrow."

The plantation foreman arrived from nearby N'Kolo at sunrise, together with two of his assistants, each of whom came equipped with large machetes. Pierre was already up and heating a kettle of water for our instant Nescafé while I dashed off to the stream to splash water on my face and change into clean shorts and shirt. When I returned, the coffee was ready and bread was shared by all five of us, accompanied by a block of cheese and slices of smoked buffalo sausage. Nothing was said about the rogue elephant.

Pierre and I then set off with the men to inspect the *cacao* trees. They stood in rows ten to fifteen feet high and were half hidden by the over-hanging branches of surrounding forest trees. "*Cacao* must have protection from the sun," explained Pierre, "and lots and lots of moisture, which the roots of these trees provide."

Gourds the shape and size of acorn squash were growing directly out of the trunks and upper main branches of the *cacao* trees. Pierre broke one off and deftly split it open with one of the worker's machetes. Inside, the gourd was packed with pods, covered with a white, sweet glistening pulp. "This pulp," he explained, "is allowed to ferment in the sun and after two days it drains away into a liquid resembling sweet cider. The beans inside the pod are exposed. And then they are dried here on bamboo mats set on trestles above the ground. For three days half the village arrives to turn them over and over in the sun. Then off they go in burlap sacks by barge to Leopoldville, by train to Matadi, then freighter to Antwerp and the *cacao* broker. Most end up in the Nestlé factory in Switzerland. It's in the factory that the roasting gets done. Once the outside skin is removed, the excess butterfat is pressed out of the beans. After that the bean is reduced to a powder and *voilà,* add a bit of sugar together with some of the butter fat, heat it up, and you have chocolate."

He rubbed the pulp off of the pod he held, exposing seeds the size and shape of almonds and the color of cinnamon. "Here. Taste one." He presented it to me with great pride. It could as well have been a nugget of gold he had just found. The seed was bitter but it definitely tasted like chocolate.

"My father would prefer coffee but *cacao* brings in more per hectare and it can be harvested all year long. But if it doesn't work out for us, Jens would be interested for his retirement. He's anxious to have my report."

I left him with the men to determine the state of health of the trees and wandered away toward an adjacent clearing in the forest singing my version of "The Big Rock Candy Mountain."

> *Oh, the buzzing of the bees*
> *And the chocolate trees,*
> *The rainbow water fountain,*
> *Where the white wine springs,*
> *And the baboon sings,*
> *On that Congo candy mountain . . .*

In the nearby clearing I discovered rows upon rows of trees as tall and straight as three-story buildings. They had slim trunks bearing no branches or vegetation. It was only toward the top that the trees sprouted a few broad leaves. Among these leaves papaya fruit was being greedily devoured by hundreds of monkeys, chattering, joyously singing to each other as they ate, swinging with the grace of trapeze artists from branch to branch, tree to tree.

Pierre found me there, standing in the middle of this ruined plantation, head back, looking up.

"Incredible," I told him. "I've never seen so many different monkeys out in the open at one time."

"It's a meeting place. They come from all over. From miles around. Nothing can discourage them. No amount of bullets can get rid of them. It's been tried, believe me."

"It's a naturalist's paradise."

"Tell that to the poor fellow who planted these. Costermans did so when the word went out that papaya produced a valuable enzyme that could be used commercially in the tenderizing of meat. He struggled for five years to keep the jungle from invading his precious garden, only to discover that when the trees finally began to bear fruit, the monkeys took over."

We left for Leopoldville at noon and hadn't gone more than a few kilometers before we met the rogue elephant again. This time face to face. He was standing in the middle of the path. A massive, towering, overwhelming cast iron-like structure, watching our approach, blocking the way. His long tusks practically swept the ground. His great fan-like ears flapped back and forth in anger. There was nowhere to go. Dense forest lined both sides of the path. Pierre gunned the motor, lay on the horn and sped forward toward the unmovable monument ahead.

Miraculously, the astonished elephant moved aside and we rushed past. I turned and looked back. Now, seething with fury, he lifted his head high and, with his trunk in the air, roared with a rage so fierce that the trumpeting echoed throughout the forest. Then he lowered his head, his formidable trunk folded up like an accordion, and came galloping at great speed after us.

"*Merde!* Son-of-a-bitch! Roll up your window!" Pierre shouted, "And hang on!"

The Renault leapt forward, practically sailing over the dirt road, rocking from side to side, stones flying out from under us peppering the undercarriage of the car, the chassis, the windshield. It seemed like an eternity before I could see in the side-view mirror that the elephant had slowed down, dropped back, turned off the path and finally disappeared into the forest.

"He's gone!" I shouted.

Pierre slowed down. Somewhat. But it wasn't until we were safely out onto the main road that he spoke, reaching out and patting my knee. "All right, *ma chère?*"

"Weew . . . . I guess so."

"I'll have to speak to the territorial administrator. This has gone too far. An elephant like that could destroy a whole village. N'Kolo is in grave danger."

"I know someone who has a gun who could solve that problem."

"Who? Soulé?"

"Yes.

"I wouldn't mess around with him if I were you." His words were curt. He wasn't just making an observation. He spoke as though he was giving me an order. Somehow Henri posed a threat to him. Could he be jealous, I wondered? This irritated me. I admired Henri and was not about to give up my friendship with him or forego our hunting expeditions.

But I didn't have a chance to reply to Pierre's criticism for at that moment a large baboon suddenly leapt out of the forest and onto the hood of the car. He banged his fist on the windshield and looked us angrily in the eye, as though demanding to be let in.

I froze. Pierre laughed. "Don't worry. He just wants a ride." And once again Pierre accelerated, faster and faster, but the baboon held on for five more miles, gripping the top of the radiator with one paw and pounding at the windshield with the other, until he decided he had had enough and jumped off.

When I asked at the bank for Henri, the new manager told me, "He's left for good. Up and quit. Said he's decided to hunt crocodiles full time. And no one's heard from him since. He's disappeared. Completely disappeared." He shook his head, lowered his voice to a conspiratorial level, thrust his face into mine, and whispered, *"They say he's got the red-eye fever."*

I stumbled out of the bank and into the blazing noonday sun that felt like so many daggers piercing my eyes, wondering why he had not said goodbye. Had he heard of my all-night foray on the Stanley Pool with Pierre or our weekend at the plantation and thought that I was no longer interested in crocodile hunting? I wondered how I could find him. And later wondered if he even wanted to be found.

# 13.

## INDEPENDENCE

T HERE WAS A hint of tears in Bill Hart's eyes when he embraced me at the airport just before he, Celeste, and his three little boys boarded the plane. Dakar needed him immediately and he couldn't wait any longer for his replacement to arrive. I would have to hold the fort until then. "I hate to leave you like this," he whispered. "There's going to be trouble."

"I'll be fine. I like this country."

Alarmed, he drew away from me, eyes wide with consternation. "All right." He understood. "But don't ever hesitate to contact me if I can help."

I squeezed his hand, which was wet with perspiration and emotion. "Thank you, dear Bill." Now there were tears in my eyes.

Ed Johnson arrived from Katmandu within a week of Bill's departure. After Tibet, he was distinctly uncomfortable in the equatorial heat of Leopoldville and kept close to the air-conditioned comfort of the consulate and his apartment in the adjoining complex. He was a shy, gentle, soft-spoken bachelor in his late forties who didn't expect to stay long. "Once this place becomes an embassy," he told me, "I'll be replaced with someone much more senior in the Agency than me." But he was a pro. After a week's orientation under my direction, I felt he could easily spare me some much-needed vacation.

Pierre telephoned me every day and stopped by my apartment in the evenings. Finally, I accepted his offer to visit his ranch in the highlands over the Christmas vacation and Ed Johnson gave me leave to go. I fell in love with the area, with Pierre, and it was there, from Bunia, that I wired my resignation from the Foreign Service. I returned to Leopoldville to collect my personal belongings and complete the necessary formalities, while Pierre stayed behind on the ranch to wait for me.

When I returned I found my replacement, Eva Mandarino, had already arrived. She had been en route to a post in Cairo, only to be told when she landed that she had to continue on to Leopoldville instead. She, too, was an old pro and, once she had recovered from the shock of having to trade metropolitan Cairo for primitive Leopoldville, she took this abrupt change in plans with great good humor and equanimity. She was especially relieved when I offered her my apartment and she promised to take good care of Claude's things. I introduced her to Maurice and he assured me he would be a good friend to her.

I also found that independence for the Belgian Congo was to become a reality at the end of six months. "June 30, 1960!" Mr. Tomlinson, the Consul General, triumphantly informed us.

There were hurried goodbye parties. Maurice arranged for the packing of my things, including my car, to be shipped by barge up the river to Stanleyville. Mr. Tomlinson convened the entire consulate staff in the conference room and, over cookies and Coke on the day prior to my departure, gave a speech wishing me well. "We're sorry to lose you and your bright smile," he said, "but going off to two plantations! We wish the very best for you. But we will miss you and your light step, rushing around, that you can hear all over the consulate. Our sunshine here. God speed. We wish you all the happiness in the world from the bottom of our hearts."

Then Larry Russell, the communications officer, announced, "Elise has something to say. Been working on the speech all night."

But all I could say was, "Thank you. Thank you very much." And something to the effect that it was ironic that I was about to lose my independence while all about me everyone else was gaining theirs.

Maurice, Ed Johnson and Eva Mandarino accompanied me to the airport. I would take the plane to Stanleyville, where I would meet Pierre, and pick up my car and belongings. Faraway Stanleyville. The place where I had first touched down in the Congo just nine months before, convinced my presence in the Belgian Congo had all been one horrible error.

Maurice took me apart from the others and led me to the balcony overlooking the runway. "I believe you will be happy," he told me, taking my hands in his, looking immensely concerned.

I realized I couldn't hide from him the doubts I had about my decision to marry. They were clearly visible in my eyes. "That makes me feel so much better," I said. "If you think so."

"I hope you will be happy. I think it is the right thing for you to do now. You went there. You saw all and still you want to marry. I believe in you." He was crying silent tears now as he said this. His face was trembling with his effort to control his emotion. He could hardly talk and I had to look away so he could finish. "You have never been disappointed in me?" he was finally able to choke out.

I couldn't speak. I, too, was choked up. I shook my head.

"And I know if you're not happy you are big enough to do something about it."

"*Oui.*"

"And always remember you are not alone in the Congo. I will always be there to help you if you ever have need of me. If something doesn't go right I am here, you know that?"

"*Oui.*"

It was then that he pulled from his pocket a small antique compass and gave it to me, saying, "That you may never lose your way."

"*Merci.*"

"And tell Pierre, too, that he can always come to me. If he needs help, I'll do all I can. *Tu sais ça?*"

"*Oui.*"

"He must know that, too. *Maintenant, embrasse-moi.*" He then held me tenderly, my cheek against his. I whispered in his ear, "Please remember for me, Maurice, you are a great and good man."

He didn't understand. So I said it again. "Yes," he blinked. "Yes. I will." He turned then and led me back to the table where Johnson and Eva were waiting. "Well, now," he tried to joke, "it's settled. It will be all right."

At the gate he tenderly kissed me once more and I told him, "Be well, Maurice. Be well."

Ed Johnson kissed me, too, and mumbled something about feeling like my father, tears coming to his eyes.

Unable to see clearly because of the tears in my own eyes, I stumbled down the field toward the waiting plane. I was amazed and profoundly grateful for the depth and strength of feeling these two men had shown for me. I had given them so little.

As I turned to wave a final goodbye, I noticed André, for whom I had bought a wife, standing on the balcony overlooking the field with this wife and their little boy. I waved at them, too, and they all waved back.

The plane followed the river again casting its shadow upon it along with those of the clouds and, from above, it appeared brown, rippled and streaked from this height with many channels between long thin islands of green.

# EPILOGUE

B ILL HART HAD been right about independence. It tore through the Congo like a series of innumerable tornadoes, touching down in rapid succession first in one part of the country and then another, ripping it apart, leaving behind devastation and ruin.

First the army mutinied, killing its Belgian officers. Out of funds, the Congolese soldiers then ransacked the banks, including the Banque du Congo Belge in Goma. I hoped that Claude, who had managed to hide out from the Germans in a hole in the woods of Belgium throughout the years of World War II, had survived. I hoped that he would live to see the fortuneteller's prediction come true.

The U.S. Embassy was besieged, as were the other new embassies, and non-essential personnel were evacuated. The marauding, leaderless Congolese army swept through the villages like crazed crocodiles, driven out of their dried-up mud holes, confiscating all arms from both natives and Europeans. When this happened to me, I was confident in my heart that there was one gun they would never have. And that was the beloved elephant gun of Henri Soulé. Surely, he would have fled over the border into Angola. He knew the way.

After this, general massacres of the white population followed throughout the country, accompanied by tribal warfare. The mighty new Congo nation splintered into many parts. Eventually I was forced to flee as well from the farm in the highlands and was evacuated to Belgium. I have already written about this period of Congolese history in my book, *The Bearded Lion Who Roars*.

Pierre and I found Maurice in Antwerp. He now lived in a tiny apartment on the third floor of a dreary apartment house hidden away on a narrow cobblestone street. It was a particularly dark and gloomy afternoon, even for Antwerp. I could barely recognize him sitting in the shadows of his living room, unsmiling, like a monument to his former self, staring vacantly at me across the tea table his distraught wife had hastily laid out with delicacies that tasted like straw to me.

"I don't know what I'm going to do with him now!" she kept moaning. "He just sits there all day. Won't go out! How am I supposed to have any fun anymore?"

I didn't plan to stay long. Maurice did not know me. For him I was already dead, along with his river and the life-giving power of the Congo sun that lesser men find unbearable. As I watched him, I knew that the heart of the great master of the Congo River had died. He would never see it again or realize his dream of retiring to a cocoa plantation. The place where he had hoped to go to his final sleep, with the perfume of the wet fertile forest in his nostrils and the sweet music of tropical song birds in his ears, knowing his inscrutable river was flowing close by. The place where his *megbe*, his shadow, would rest in the village of the dead, while a magnificent insect from the forest with shimmering, iridescent wings would carry his soul up to the Supreme Being. It would surely have to be a special kind of insect to transport so great a soul as that of Captain Maurice Jens. A blue and golden butterfly, perhaps.

Suddenly, he spoke to me asking, "And now what are you going to do?"

"We're going back."

"To New York?"

"No. To the Congo."

"And do what?"

"To see what we can see," Pierre replied. "Save what we can save of the farm. When things settle down, of course. It's crazy, I know, but it's something we have to do."

Maurice rose to his feet, sunlight spreading across his wide countenance, defying the gloom of the room. He held his arms out wide to me and I went into his embrace. His last words were, "Then there is hope!"

But things never did "settle down" enough for me to return. Pierre did go back, though. Briefly. On October 5, 1960, he returned to the Congo when the press reported that things were calming down in the interior, that the madness of the mutinous Congolese army had run its course and that UN troops had things under control. I could not join him, though, for I was pregnant and remained in Belgium to await the birth of our first child.

After many misadventures Pierre finally managed to reach our farm. The Army had made off with half our cattle but our workers were still there, running it as best they could. Realizing the situation was hopeless, Pierre turned everything over to our personnel, organizing it as a cooperative and putting our headman in charge.

Since then I find myself, from time to time, telling the tale of the man I once knew who could speak to hippopotamuses. People listen politely to my stories. Children, especially, like to hear me repeat this tale. But I doubt if they believe me.

I often think of Henri, as well. The man with the red-eye fever. The children like to hear this story, too. How together we slew the dragon of the Kwango—El Diablo. I always wonder what happened to Henri. And at the same time I know that I will never know.

# ABOUT THE AUTHOR

B ORN ELISE CAMILLE Cookson in Tarrytown, New York, 1933, Elise grew up in neighboring Peekskill, New York. Her varied career, spanning five decades, has taken her to many countries on four continents, including the South Seas before the advent of jet travel. She practiced a wide variety of professions ranging from independent film producer in Hollywood to farmer in Africa and Argentina to Wall Street broker and public school foreign language teacher, until finally, at age sixty-one, she was able to begin her writing career.

Beginning in Europe in 1955, she was hired as a publicist for a motion picture company. From there she went on to work in Hollywood, New York, and on location for major motion pictures. After Hollywood, she joined the U.S. Foreign Service and was assigned to the Belgian Congo, where she met her explorer husband, Pierre Dallemagne. She managed his family's ranch and coffee plantation until the Congo's independence forced them out. Her first book, *The Bearded Lion Who Roars*, a memoir published in 1995, recounts what happened during those historic times.

From the Congo she and her husband immigrated to

Argentina, where they established a dairy farm. Her first novel, *The Ombú Tree*, published in 1998, is based on her experiences farming in that country. It is the tale of a modern-day American woman pioneer on the pampas, confronting revolution and frontier justice as she attempts to wrest a successful farm out of a haunted estancia surrounded by a network of Nazi neighbors.

*The Filmmaker*, her second novel published in 2000, is the tragic love story about an Academy-Award-winning filmmaker who became a victim of "McCarthyism" and subsequently "named names" of former Communist Party colleagues before the House Un-American Activities Committee.

With *The Red-Eye Fever*, Elise Dallemagne-Cookson recounts tales of her adventures hunting crocodiles in the former Belgian Congo before it became independent in 1960 and introduces us to some extraordinary people she met at that time.

Printed in the United States
1205200001B/17-24